THE TAO OF TREK

James T. Lambert

JAMES T LAMBERT
TROY LAMBERT

Boldly go!

ML
MOONEY &
LAMBERT

PRINT ISBN: 9780578392585

"A man either lives life as it happens to him, meets it head-on and licks it, or he turns his back on it and starts to wither away."

— Dr. Boyce, "The Menagerie," Gene Roddenberry

"This is a new land, this is a new place, this is a new world, this is unknown. This is uncharted, this is all there is. We don't have any other place to go. I always quote Gene as saying, 'Why are we now going into space? Well, why did we trouble to look past the next mountain? Our prime obligation to ourselves is to make the unknown known. We are on a journey to keep an appointment with whatever we are.' And that was his whole philosophy of Star Trek, of life, of everything else."

— Majel Barrett Roddenberry, 1994 Jim Plaxco interview

AUTHORS' NOTES

This book is written by two authors, both Trekkies. James T. Lambert is not a pen name: that is "Jim's" actual name. And Troy is a sci-fi kid who grew up to write mysteries. Below, you'll find both of our notes to you, the reader, explaining a little bit about who we are.

Throughout the book, we will use the pronouns "we" and "I". We simply mean this is something we both agree on. When we use "I" every attempt will be made to identify the speaker, but if you are confused, feel free to reach out, or to ask us at your favorite conference.

We look forward to seeing you out there. With that, it's time for introductions.

James T. Lambert

I'm a *Star Trek* kid. While born a little late to catch the original series pilot episode — and too young to appreciate the first run on network TV — I watched avidly as it took off in syndication. Long before our first VCR, I'd watched every episode featuring Kirk, Spock, McCoy, Scotty, Uhura, Sulu, and Chekov.

Sure, I enjoyed other series. *Space 1999, UFO, Ultraman,* and *Thunderbirds* played regularly, but I bought the *Star Trek* Technical Manual and models of the landing party gear (phaser, communicator, and tricorder). I watched *Battlestar Galactica* (the original one!) and even bought models of the Cylon fighter and the Viper, but I went to *Star Trek* conventions.

I saw the infamous blooper reel before its theft. I heard Jimmy Doohan talk about his experience recording a voice for a Warner Bros cartoon and getting in trouble for doing too many of the voices. I attended a convention where Bjo Trimble did a reverse signing. We all signed a banner for the guests instead of them signing items for us. She and her husband ran the letter-writing campaign to get a third season of the original series after the studio announced its cancellation after the second season.

I knew the difference between a Trekkie and a Trekker.

Star Trek was my thing.

And not just mine. As time went by, I met others who loved *Star Trek* and joined a local club dedicated to just *Star Trek*. I met a fellow community theater actor who'd been at that same convention where Jimmy Doohan appeared (may he Rest in Peace), but with a better story. Younger than me, he'd waited in line a long time to get a signature from 'Scotty', getting more and more excited. At the front of the line, at last, he vomited. "I bet he remembers me," he said. At a recent convention (where William Shatner and several *Next Generation* actors attended), I ran into a coworker in a skant uniform (The name of the uniform type, not that she was scantily clad) from the original series.

So many people have invested so much of their lives in *Star Trek*. And even if the newest *Star Trek* stories aren't the same as the ones from the sixties, I realize how much the world took from *Star Trek* and how much *Star Trek* took from the world. With

Gene Roddenberry's 100th just passed, I wanted to look back on how *Star Trek* influenced people's lives and beliefs. What ideas popularized by this series are now common cultural currency. How the way of belief, the Tao, in *Star Trek* leaked out into its viewers before spreading even further.

How the *Tao of Star Trek* changed the world.

James T. "Jim" Lambert

2022

Troy Lambert

It was 2013, and I'd just moved back to what I call my "boomerang city" of Boise, Idaho. My first time at a writer's group, everyone went around and introduced themselves. Before things got around to me, a writer with a fabulous beard and an infectious laugh introduced himself: "Jim Lambert."

We checked. We're not related, but we look like we could be. We joke that we've been married, but not to each other. And we've been friends ever since. Jim writes sci-fi and some really great steampunk stuff. I write mysteries, thrillers, and stuff that is a little...darker. However, I grew up as a sci-fi kid. My Uncle Harold was a huge Trekkie, and I followed in his footsteps. I watched the entire original series in reruns over many afternoons at our babysitter's house. When mom would show up early, and I would miss the end of an episode, it often caused great anxiety until I was able to find out what happened. Season 1, Episode 8 (Miri) is but one example. I had nightmares, worried that Kirk would die (although as the series was in syndication, you would think I would have realized he had to have lived).

I also remember my first *Star Trek* convention. My Uncle took me to a hotel in Richland, Washington, and I could see several versions of Mr. Spock as soon as I entered the lobby. I'd never seen or even heard of Cosplay at that point--but I knew these were fans. No matter who you were, you were welcome if you liked Star Trek.

I watched the television series, loved the films (although we weren't allowed to go to theaters in our family, so after they came out on video at that time). *Wrath of Kahn* changed me like I think it changed all of us Trekkies at the time. And then...

Well then, I grew up. I learned that Trek meant more than just a cool world. I mean, I KNEW that. Sci-fi changed the way I think--frankly, it saved me, and while I may share a bit of that here, that story is more fit for another book another time. I read the books, as many as my library let me get my hands on. I followed the *Next Generation* as I spawned my own *Next Generation* – er, had kids. *Discovery* came along as I discovered more about who I was.

Now, we stream the films. We read books that base their leadership styles on Jean-Luc Picard. As fans, we write fanfic, sing songs, and bemoan the horror of some of the recent films (we're looking at you, JJ).

But as I look back, I see the thread of *Star Trek* through my life. And I wonder: would my life have been the same without it? Would I have learned some of the lessons I have without the leadership of Kirk, the wisdom of Spock, and the philosophy, dare I say, *The Tao of Trek*? I don't think so.

In fact, I think *Star Trek* changed the world. This book, written with one of my best friends in the world, one who shares more than just a love of Trek, is our attempt to chronicle that philosophy and the how and why things have changed.

So, open your mind as you open this book, and journey with us as we boldly go...

You know the rest.

Troy Lambert

2021

INTRODUCTION: THE BIRTH OF THE TAO OF TREK

"PICARD: There is no greater challenge than the study of philosophy.

WESLEY: But William James won't be in my Starfleet exams.

PICARD: The important things never will be. Anyone can be trained in the mechanics of piloting a starship.

WESLEY: But Starfleet Academy

PICARD: It takes more. Open your mind to the past. Art, history, philosophy. And all this may mean something."

— *Robert L. McCullough, Next Generation Season 2, Episode 17,*
"Samaritan Snare"

Troy: I don't remember the Stardate, but I remember entering the lobby of the quite swanky, at least by my family's standards, Red Lion in Kennewick, Washington. As the doors whooshed shut behind me, a Klingon walked by, chatting with Mr. Spock. Mr. Spock? Illogical.

Yet there he was. They were followed rapidly by a group of red shirts and a gorgeous Lt. Uhura. I didn't know then that there was a philosophy, a whole world behind *Star Trek*. I just knew that when I watched *Star Trek*, when I got a few of the books in my hands, I felt like I was transported to another world.

You see, *Star Trek* took me to a place quite different from the world of my young existence. The crew had a food replicator. There were a lot of potatoes in our house, and some nights when fried bologna served as the cornerstone to yet another course of au gratin, fried spuds, or mashed potatoes drowned in cheap catsup. If we were lucky, the meal was accompanied by a frozen veggie or something home canned the previous fall. *Star Trek* was a world of plenty, one where you didn't have to wrangle an invitation from your friend for a sleepover so you could get a bowl of the "good cereal." Ours was a world of wants and wishes. We didn't starve, but we knew sometimes that was a struggle for our mom.

From the introduction of each episode, outlining the crew's mission to "seek out new worlds and new civilizations, to boldly go where no man had gone before" to the very idea of the Prime Directive, the idea of taking care not to harm other civilizations and their development by introducing new, more advanced technology, the crew of the *Enterprise*, under the capable, but arguably overacted leadership of Captain Kirk, seemed intent on doing the right thing.

I wanted to follow them, not only on their five-year mission but in my own peaceful exploration of the world around me. The older I got, the more I realized *Star Trek* was much deeper and had a more significant impact on me, and on others who were fans of the franchise, from Trekkies to casual watchers, than I at first imagined.

The Tao of Trek is an organized exploration of that philosophy. Why Tao? Because Tao is defined as the absolute principle underlying the universe, combining within itself the principles of yin and yang and signifying the way, or code of behavior, that is in harmony with the natural order of things. Tao itself is not a religion, although religions have developed around it, including the interpretation of Tao in the Tao-te-Ching that evolved into the philosophical religion of Taoism.

And in a large way, *Star Trek* contains similar absolute principles through the Prime Directive and other moral principles. The Federation seeks to work only "with the natural order and harmony of things." Over the years, this underlying philosophy has been adopted and even studied by Trekkies the world over. In fact, we see clear parallels between Buddhism and the Tao of Trek.

BUDDHISM AND *THE TAO OF TREK*

Maybe the aspirational ideal of Trek would simply be this: That just because someone is different does not mean they are evil. This is clearly illustrated in TOS Season 1, Episode 25, titled simply "The Devil in the Dark." While Spock and Kirk battle a subterranean creature that has killed humans, they discover a chamber filled with silicon modules Spock (through a mind-meld) learns are the creature's eggs.

The hostility came from a "mother" protecting her young, and young that were only produced every 5,000 years. Her very civilization was at stake. You could even say that her actions were intended to sacrifice the needs of the few for the good of the many.

Just because the creature's actions were hostile did not mean the creature itself had some kind of hostile intent. In fact, its acts were in self-defense. The point was that simply because we as humans didn't understand them did not mean we were inherently "right."

We see this today in our large political divides and polarization. Just because someone sees the world differently does not mean they are "the enemy" or "evil" even if we feel they are "wrong." Of course, this is a hard thing for anyone to balance, but often to achieve peace, one must back away and take a larger view of the situation.

This very principle is expressed in the Buddhist philosophy and most directly in the principle of non-attachment and achieving enlightenment.

Think of it this way, when we break down the four simple truths of Buddhism and relate them to Trek. Before we get there, we must understand the way the two systems overlap.

The Tao Exists No Matter Who the Captain Is

Just as buddhism exists outside of any one individual or supreme leader, so the Tao exists outside any one captain. Even the Buddha himself was simply a vehicle for a message of truth and pointed his followers toward other religious leaders and teachings as well. We do not need Picard or Kirk or any other leader to show us that peaceful exploration and the lack of war is a good thing. We'll explore this in detail in the second part of this book.

The Good of the Many Outweighs the Needs of the Few or the One

The biggest cause of suffering, according to Buddhism, is attachment. Wars are a result of a more global attachment of society to something: a principle, a piece of land, etc. However, enlightenment shows us that we are all unified, and there is no reason to be attached to those things, as a people or as individuals. Therefore, war and the suffering that comes with it are useless.

In the case of the Devil in the Dark, the creature was attached to her young - not a bad thing, but the other inhabitants of the planet were attached to their right to mine and occupy the tunnels that made up her home. If either of them were to take a moment to look at the absurdity of their attachments, they would be able to live in unity.

Religion isn't Essential

In the Buddhist religion, beliefs are not controlled. In fact, you can believe anything you want as a Buddhist and are encouraged to do so in the search for enlightenment. Although many Buddhists believe in reincarnation, not all do. There are many different belief systems in Buddhism.

The same is true of Trek and the Tao that arises out of it. While we often think of *Star Trek* as areligious, there are many examples of religion in the series. Most often, at least early on, these are associated with less advanced alien species.

But in *Deep Space 9, The Next Generation*, and specifically in *Discovery*, there are frequent religious references throughout the episodes. We'll explore these throughout this work as well.

This leads to the four spiritual truths of the Tao of Trek, as related to those of Buddhism:

#1: Beyond the Five-Year Mission

No matter what happens, the *Enterprise* keeps moving forward in its mission. Even if a crew member dies or a shuttle is lost or damaged, the journey goes on.

In Buddhism, this cycle is often expressed as "life is suffering." But again, suffering is not what you think. It's the Pali word dukkha, which refers to anything that is temporary, conditional, or compounded of other things.

In other words, even if something is pleasurable, it is temporary, and it is important to not get too attached. Because we are all on a lifelong mission and there is no time for stopping or undue attachments to any one person or place.

#2: Post-Scarcity

What if you could have everything you need, all the time? What if there was nothing you really need that you couldn't get by simply existing the way you were designed to? Well, even in today's world, you can.

You see, we don't need to look for happiness in anything outside of ourselves. The source of our happiness is within each and every one of us. As long as our essential human needs are met, there is no need for seeking more.

And in the world of post-scarcity *Star Trek*, everything the crew needs is available. Scarcity, or even the false perception of it, does not drive greed. The exceptions are rare cases in other species or in specific environments where scarcity is a risk (*DS9* and in some instances *Discovery*).

#3: Live Long and Prosper

What if you could achieve enlightenment and move beyond the need for attachment and the search for happiness outside of yourself? The good news is, you can.

The Buddha teaches that with mindful practice, you can put an end to craving, and thus achieve enlightenment. The Vulcan philosophy tells us the same: we can live long and prosper through developing our mental strength, embracing logic over emotion, and reminding ourselves of the true meaning of Tao.

Non-attachment, peace with others, and an understanding of how temporary this life is will lead us to greet everyone with the sentiment: "Live Long and Prosper."

#4: The Starfleet Academy

Enlightenment doesn't happen accidentally. It comes through training. In Buddhism, this is the eightfold path to enlightenment. For those of Starfleet, it starts at the Starfleet Academy.

However, it doesn't stop there. Our learning is always continuing, and while we may never beat the Kobayashi Maru, we can get closer, better, and eventually achieve the enlightenment we need to truly live the *Tao of Trek*.

There are other ways that Buddhism intersects with Trek as well, and we look at those in more detail on our blog from time to time. Suffice it to say that on this topic, the very principles of Buddhism make war an unnecessary evil. (22)

We must take a moment here, however, to say something about religion: there are extremists in any belief system. They become so attached to the idea of being "right" that they are willing to go to war to defend those principles.

Which is, in principle, a violation of their religion. Buddhism is no exception, and while we won't go into those details here, it is important that we state we are not talking about extremism in any way when we refer to religious parallels with the Tao of Trek. Instead, we are referring to the Sanskrit word *samyanc,* which means "wholesome" or "ideal."

In that way, we also want to talk about how Star Trek and its ideals inspire conversations.

INSPIRING CONVERSATIONS ABOUT REAL ISSUES

Despite being pure fiction, *Star Trek* used certain ideas in its storytelling and promoted them among its fandom in the real world. Ways of thinking, beliefs, social structures, and even gestures and phrases became well known among fans of the series. As time went on, these spread further afield, joining our culture's conversation even between groups never associated with the show.

Of course, most of these ideas initially filtered into *Star Trek* through scripts and books, coming from beliefs in the outside world. Still, the added emphasis from adopting these ideas and their redistribution through its popularity cannot be understated.

Star Trek was a product of its time. The sixties, known for hippies and free love, also fostered anti-war protests, civil rights, and the space race. Many of these movements appeared in *Star Trek* in various forms. With the backdrop of the many injustices apparent at the time, seeing a Utopian future depicted on-screen appealed to many viewers.

While Gene Roddenberry pitched the idea as a space western, calling it "Wagon Train to the Stars", he planned for episodic stories with disguised moral underpinnings. While the plot told an exciting story pitting the crew of the Enterprise against a variety of situations, on a deeper level, these illustrated contemporary conflicts regarding war, race, gender, sex, religion, and politics.

THE ROLE OF ENTERTAINMENT

While we love to talk about the value of *Star Trek* as a philosophical work and having an impact on our culture, the original purpose was, of course, entertainment. To understand the show's origins, it's important to understand where Roddenberry himself was at the time.

By the mid-1960s, Gene Roddenberry was a reasonably successful producer who had not only written and produced several episodes for television but had also written and pitched his own series and scripts. He had some controversial ideas and even quit series and lost friends over them. In fact, when he was asked to write for a series titled *Riverboat*, he lost his chance when he protested the fact that the network didn't want any black people on the show.

But his show, *The Lieutenant*, which included many of the stars who would later join him for *Star Trek*, was a critical success, setting ratings records for its Saturday timeslot. He clashed with the Pentagon, who allowed the show to be filmed on an actual Marine base, several times over plots, and the final straw was the plot titled "To Set it Right" in which a white and a black man found common cause in their role as Marines. The show lasted one season and was not renewed. That episode, however, is preserved in the Museum of Television and was the television debut of Nichelle Nichols.

Once it was canceled, he revived two ideas he'd had before, one of an airship that traveled around the world with a multi-ethnic crew (one he'd come up with in 1961) and a series set on a cruise ship that he'd pitched to CBS in 1956. He added a "Horatio Hornblower" character (Kirk) and decided to set it in space. What we now know as *Star Trek* started as a 16-page pitch sent to the Writer's Guild of America in April of 1964, accompanied by the $2 fee to register the series.

While Roddenberry wanted to and did explore controversial themes, his primary goal was, of course, to sell series and make money. So, he pitched it to MGM, where it got a "warm reception" but they didn't make an offer. Undaunted, he took it to Desilu Productions, who were in an interesting position. Their only real success had been *The Lucy Show*, they hadn't sold a pilot in quite a while, and so they hired him as a producer with the freedom to create his own shows. After a few other pitches, Roddenberry teamed up with Oliver Katz, then head of Desilu, to try to sell the series. CBS passed, but after some work, NBC picked it up, announcing the premiere as part of the 1966 lineup.

Gene Roddenberry appeared at The World Science Fiction convention in September 1966, a few days before the first episode aired on NBC, and premiered "Where No Man Has Gone Before." A new cult of fans was born.

Many Trekkies had yet to be born, and little did Roddenberry or even early fans know that the world was changed that day. What would become one of the most acclaimed series on the big and small screen started with a whimper rather than a bang, but as we will see as we explore television history, that whimper soon became a roar that could not be ignored.

It all started with ideas. Roddenberry explored ideas of right and wrong, inclusiveness, and a brave new world. But he did it all to entertain us, and he succeeded.

THE ROAD AHEAD

We're going to examine the Tao of Trek in two parts: in the first part, we will look at the background of Trek and give you an overview of the show. If you are a Trekkie well-versed in the universe, you can skip parts of this section: if you know the origin of the show, what constitutes cannon, and the timeline of both the creation and release of the various series and the Stardate timeline itself, you can pretty much skip volume one, or pick and choose the sections you want to read.

We will also talk in the first section about the cast. The stars of the original series, Leonard Nimoy and William Shatner, were both sons of Ukrainian Jewish immigrants. Both grew up in kosher homes, and both were taunted by anti-Semitic slurs growing up.

"Experiences like that create a sort of subtext," Shatner wrote in *Leonard: My Fifty-Year Friendship With a Remarkable Man*, his 2016 book, "and as we got to know each other, those common experiences helped bind us together. It's almost an emotional shorthand."

We also discuss not only the timeline of Trek, but how the timing of each show and its place in the canon helped communicate these values to the world. We'll also talk about how revisionism is not always a bad thing: *The Tao of Trek* has evolved and will continue to do so, and we'll examine the very idea of an evolving canon that originated with Gene Roddenberry himself.

We will also take a glance into the world of bards and minstrels, those who write (and sing) about *Star Trek* outside the traditional framework of the small and large screen. We'll talk about fan works (like this book), official guides, and more, along with some of the trek-inspired songs that are a part of the filk circuit (a version of folk singing we will discuss later) found at conventions, meetings, and even lesser-known albums.

Finally, before we step into the second part of the book, we will talk about cons: how Trek shaped fandom and the way people celebrate together, and how in the subsequent years, cons have impacted Trek and Trekkies.

Then in volume two, we're going to take a systematic, dare we say "religious" approach to this non-religious philosophy followed by Trekkies and informally called Trekkism. First, we will look at the audacity of *Star Trek* and the willingness to "boldly go" in so many ways. Then we will tackle, from a fan perspective as well as a more formal one, some deeper topics.

- **The Prime Directive:** The sovereignty of every planet and civilization is born out of a desire to not interfere with another culture. But is it really the moral high ground, or should the Federation step in and share their knowledge to improve the future of those they encounter and perhaps save them? The answer is tougher than you think.

- **To Boldly Go:** The original series pioneered some principles on the small screen and later on the big screen as well. It was a bold move, mirroring the mission statement in the opening credits. In what ways did Trek, and is Trek, still doing this?
- **Infinite Diversity in Infinite Combinations:** Where did this come from? What does it mean in terms of diversity, racism, and other topics? How has Trek done this well, and where has it failed?
- **Freedom from Religion:** Is Star Trek really areligious? In what ways? Is that a good or a bad thing?
- **Post Scarcity and Kindness:** How does the lack of poverty and need, at least in the Federation, change the underlying goals and desires for both individuals and groups? What does it mean to other races (like the Klingons) who face poverty and need in contrast to the Federation? How does that mirror our society and our world today?
- **Meaningful Work:** We live in a world where make-work jobs that have no meaning are commonplace. But is there such a thing on a starship? Is there any room for such things in the openness of space? Even *Star Trek: Lower Decks* shows us that every person, every job has a place and a purpose. How does that compare to where we are today, and how can we make changes to align with this truth?
- **The Good of the Many:** *Star Trek* is filled with examples of personal sacrifice of one for the good of the many, perhaps one of the best examples coming in *Wrath of Kahn*. How does this spirit of sacrifice and the ultimate kindness pervade the show, the *Star Trek* world, and what does it mean to us today?

- **War, What is it Good For:** Peaceful exploration and the desire to avoid war with things like the neutral zone, various treaties, and the Federation itself make the foundation of *Star Trek*. And even though wars happen in the overall timeline (what is a story without conflict?), the ultimate desire is universal peace. What can we learn from this philosophy?
- **Live Long and Prosper:** Where did this come from? What does the Vulcan hand sign really mean? Why is this greeting so meaningful? Where does this fit in the later *Star Trek* universe, and how does it apply to our lives as Taoists of Trek?
- **Not Your Grandfather's Trek:** Okay, we all heard the quote when the film *Star Trek* was advertised, but what about the controversial and polarizing Kelvin Timeline? What did it do to the overall Tao of Trek? Even though it brought in new fans, did it do so in the right way? Did the subsequent films bring Trek back to its roots?
- **The Trek of Tomorrow:** It is an exciting time to be a Trekkie, and there are many things happening in the franchise. What does the future look like from the perspective of fans, both old and young? How will the franchise be seen by the *Next Generation*?

For the authors, *The Tao of Trek* is about more than just the events in the *Star Trek* films, episodes, and even books and other work. Instead, it is about what those things mean, what we can learn from them, and why they are important.

With that out of the way, let's dive into Part One.

PART ONE
THE TIMELINE, BACKGROUND, CAST, AND FANS OF STAR TREK

"They used to say that if man was meant to fly, he'd have wings. But he did fly. He discovered he had to."

- Captain James T Kirk

"We are here today to re-christen the USS Enterprise and to honor those who lost their lives nearly one year ago. When Christopher Pike first gave me his ship, he had me recite the Captain's Oath. Words I didn't appreciate at the time. Now I see them as a call for us to remember who we once were and who we must be again. And those words? Space... the final frontier. These are the voyages of the Starship Enterprise, her five-year mission to explore strange new worlds, to seek out new life and new civilizations. To boldly go where no one has gone before."

- Captain James T Kirk

Since we'll be using the names of the various Star Trek series and films a lot, we'll probably drop into the commonly used abbreviations for them. Wikipedia has conveniently aggregated these for us, so with grateful thanks, we'll be using their list. Please donate to Wikipedia (James: I did!) to help them continue their fine work.

- TOS   Star Trek: The Original Series (1966–1969)
- TAS   Star Trek: The Animated Series (1973–1974)
- TMP   Star Trek: The Motion Picture (1979)
- WOK   Star Trek II: The Wrath of Khan (1982)
- TSFS   Star Trek III: The Search for Spock (1984)
- TVH   Star Trek IV: The Voyage Home (1986)
- TFF   Star Trek V: The Final Frontier (1989)
- TUC   Star Trek VI: The Undiscovered Country (1991)
- TNG   Star Trek: The Next Generation (1987–1994)
- DS9   Star Trek: Deep Space Nine (1993–1999)
- GEN   Star Trek Generations (1994)
- VOY   Star Trek: Voyager (1995–2001)
- FC   Star Trek: First Contact (1996)
- INS   Star Trek: Insurrection (1998)
- NEM   Star Trek: Nemesis (2002)
- ENT   Star Trek: Enterprise (2001–2005)
- ST09   Star Trek (2009)
- STID   Star Trek Into Darkness (2013)
- STB   Star Trek Beyond (2016)
- DIS   Star Trek: Discovery (2017–present)
- SHO   Star Trek: Short Treks (2018–2020)
- PIC   Star Trek: Picard (2020–present)
- LOW   Star Trek: Lower Decks (2020–present)
- PRO   Star Trek: Prodigy (2021–present)
- SNW   Star Trek: Strange New Worlds (2022–present)

CHAPTER 1
THE GENERAL TIMELINE

"This is space. It's sometimes called the final frontier.

(Except that of course you can't have a final frontier, because there'd be nothing for it to be a frontier to, but as frontiers go, it's pretty penultimate . . .)"

— Terry Pratchett, *Moving Pictures*

"Why a journey into space? Because science is now learning that the infinite reaches of our universe probably teem with as much life and adventure as Earth's own oceans and continents. Our galaxy alone is so incredibly vast that the most conservative mathematical odds still add up to millions of planets almost identical to our own — capable of life, even intelligence, and strange new civilizations. Alien beings that will range from the fiercely primitive to the incredibly exotic intelligence which will far surpass Mankind. (The Hollywood Reporter, Sept. 8, 1966)"

— Gene Roddenberry

"You want to know the problem with going somewhere no one's ever been? It takes so damned long to get there."

— *Dayton Ward, Armageddon's Arrow*

There are two (well, technically three, but we will get there) things we talk about when we say "timeline" and "*Star Trek*" in the same sentence. One is the timeline of the shows in our timeline and when and how they were released (and will be released, as this is an ongoing timeline). The other is the actual "historical" timeline in the show. This is, of course, illustrated well in *First Contact (FC)* when we see the moment that the warp drive became an essential part of human evolution and the beginning of our journey to the stars and beyond.

For the sake of our discussion, we will talk first about the physical release of the various parts of the franchise in our timeline. Rather than talking about the show by decade, we are going to use what have become the accepted eras of the show:

- The original series era: 1965-1969
- The post original series rebirth: 1969-1991 (this is when I first became a Trekkie)
- Post Roddenberry television era: 1991-2005
- Rebooted film series: 2005-2016
- Expansion of the *Star Trek* Universe: 2017-Present

Finally, the future of *Star Trek* on the big and small screen, which we will deal with more fully in the final chapter of this book.

We will look at each of these quickly: if you are reading this and you are a Trekkie (and it is likely that you are), this will be a good refresher for you, but if you are already intimately familiar with the timeline, you can skip this chapter and get to the more philosophical bits. If you are new to the franchise, this can serve as a binge guide, but set aside some time. There are a lot of hours of Trek to consume.

With that, let's get started:

THE ORIGINAL SERIES ERA: 1964-1969

As we have stated previously, *Star Trek* was a product of its time. The sixties fostered many social changes, and several appeared in *Star Trek* in various forms. This was the time for shows that depicted the kind of future *Star Trek* promised. The plot told an exciting story of the crew of the Enterprise in a variety of situations that illustrated contemporary conflicts regarding war, sex, religion, and politics.

After creating the original pilot episode, "The Cage", in 1965, NBC turned it down as too intellectual for their audience. In an unusual decision, they commissioned a second pilot, "Where No Man Has Gone Before". After accepting this revision, the show ran for two seasons and received high ratings, although they declined as time went on. As a result, Paramount threatened to cancel the show at the end of the second, which mobilized the fan base.

Led by Bjo Trimble, a letter-writing campaign (primarily fueled by female fans) caused the network to renew the show for a third season. Unfortunately, resistance to the renewal moved the show out of primetime to a dreaded Friday slot and reduced the filming budget. Ratings suffered, and despite a second letter-writing campaign, the fans' pleas failed to secure a fourth season, and *Star Trek* TOS ended with only 79 episodes, the last of which aired June 3rd, 1969.

Surprisingly, the syndication release of *Star Trek* began the same year, and many stations saw an increase in their ratings due to it. Over time, TOS gained wide popularity through its syndication, gathering even more fans than it had during its initial broadcasts. That led to a rebirth in the 1970s.

THE POST ORIGINAL SERIES REBIRTH: 1969-1991

As we entered a new decade where humanity had reached the moon, *Star Trek* continued to gain popularity in syndication. One indication of its increased fan base came with the first *Star Trek* convention, held January 21-23, 1972. While organizers planned for only a few hundred attendees, over three thousand fans showed up. We'll discuss conventions, which still continue to this day, later in the book.

With such an enthusiastic viewership eager for more *Star Trek*, a new animated series was created and ran from 1973 to 1974. *Star Trek: The Animated Series* (TAS) went on to win an Emmy Award for Outstanding Entertainment: Children's Series. Things were looking up for the franchise. Development of a new series, *Star Trek*: Phase II, was well underway in May 1975 but stopped suddenly when Paramount Pictures scrapped their offshoot Paramount Television Service, which had been working with Roddenberry on the series.

Surprisingly, while no television series to replace Phase II were planned, *Star Trek* made the leap to the big screen. Due to the success of science fiction films such as *Star Wars* and *Close Encounters of the Third Kind*, *Star Trek* got a new lease on life. Recycling parts of the pilot episode for Phase II into a feature film, Paramount released *Star Trek: The Motion Picture* (TMP) in December of 1979, ending the seventies with a clear win.

During the eighties, four additional *Star Trek* films were released. The second in the series, *Star Trek II: The Wrath of Kahn* (WoK), is often seen as one of the best Trek film adaptations of all time. While *TMP* stood alone, WoK was the first of a series of three films that followed a single storyline. While each film stands alone, together they tell the story of the death of Spock, his miraculous resurrection (*The Search for Spock*), and the crew of the Enterprise's final *Voyage Home*, another fantastic film showcasing the philosophy of *Star Trek* in stellar fashion (pardon the pun).

Right before the release of *The Voyage Home*, the follow-on series, The *Next Generation*, made its television debut in 1987.

In that way, the 1980s were a busy time and ended on both a high and a low note. *The Next Generation (TNG)* was quickly adopted and followed by Trek fans. *The Final Frontier*, however, was a critical and financial flop, and it seemed like the days of *TOS* on the big screen might just be over.

The 1990s started off on the same sour note that the 1980s ended on: despite the lukewarm success of *The Final Frontier*, the next film *The Undiscovered Country* was already in production and set to debut in 1991. Roddenberry screened the film prior to its release and had some interesting thoughts on it, although likely we will never know precisely what those were. That's because shortly after the screening, but before the film was released, Roddenberry passed away at the ripe young age of seventy. On October 24, 1991, *Star Trek* entered the post-Roddenberry-inspired era.

POST-RODDENBERRY TELEVISION ERA: 1991-2005

Following Roddenberry's death, *Star Trek* continued to rise in popularity. TNG continued to gather fans, and a spin-off series, *Deep Space 9* (DS9), was released in 1993. When TNG was canceled after seven seasons (in 1995) another series, *Voyager* (VOY), was released. The mid-1990s marked the height of *Star Trek*'s popularity, with DS9 and VOY airing simultaneously.

In addition, the real reason *The Next Generation* was canceled was to take the success of the series to the big screen. This happened with four films, three of which would air in the 1990s:

- *Generations* (A crossover with TOS) 1994
- *First Contact* 1996
- *Insurrection* 1998

When relating to *The Tao of Trek*, it is important to recognize just how much *Star Trek* had entered the mainstream of society. Those who were introduced to the series with Captain Picard and TNG often went back and revisited TOS, now in common syndication and available in all kinds of at-home video formats, including special editions.

While we had not yet entered the age of streaming, and the internet was a pretty new thing, there were bulletin boards and chat groups related to *Star Trek*, and conventions were going strong, drawing more numbers than ever, with more character costumes, including Klingons, Romulans, and other less familiar species.

Despite his rocky start in Season One of TNG, Picard began to take his place as a role model and a captain of his own, on par with, and some would argue superior to Kirk.

This nearly golden decade for the franchise, which became the most important property to Paramount at the time, was about to face some uncertainty going into the 2000s.

When *Voyager* ended, a prequel series titled *Enterprise (ENT)* first aired in 2001, it served as the anchor for the flagship Universal Paramount Network. But the series did not fare as well as expected, and after three seasons, UPN was set to cancel it. But a fan campaign like the one that brought TOS back for another season was mounted, and the show was renewed for one more season but moved it to what was known at the time as the "Friday Night Death Spot."

A fan group calling themselves "Save Enterprise" tried and failed to resurrect the series, even attempting to privately raise funds to cover production costs. The film *Nemesis* failed to perform well at the box office in 2002 when it was released, and the cancellation of ENT ended 18 years of continuous *Star Trek* television production.

But 2005 brought a new birth for the series, sort of.

THE REBOOTED FILM SERIES: 2005-2016

The parent company of Paramount, Viacom, split into two different companies, CBS Corporation which owned CBS Television Studios, and Viacom, which took over ownership of Paramount Pictures. So, while one company held rights to the television franchise, another held the rights to the films and would also continue the production of the film franchise.

In 2007 Viacom hired a new team which included JJ Abrams to revitalize the series, creating films on what would later be known as the Kelvin Timeline. Creating the films as a prequel to the TOS with a different cast playing the roles of the original characters meant they could operate outside the original canon. The eleventh film overall, simply called *Star Trek*, was deliberately marketed to groups who were fans of sci-fi, but not necessarily of the Trek franchise.

The film debuted in 2009 and received a lukewarm response that, at best, polarized fans. "I genuinely still believe that the 2009 *Star Trek* is one of the stupidest movies I have seen in my entire life," Arnold Blumberg, University of Baltimore media studies professor and *Star Trek* aficionado, told *Vulture* in 2013. "That movie is awful on almost every conceivable level. The plot, the structure of the film, the characterization, the action set pieces — it's one of the rare occasions I've ever sat through a movie where I felt it was insulting my intelligence at every turn."

He was not alone. Many Trek fans felt Abrams did a horrible job on the first film and declared it did not live up to the intelligence, spirit, and scope of the original. "The entire plot hinges on one of the silliest McGuffins in cinematic history, this 'red matter' that basically does whatever they want it to do, whenever they want it to do it, in contradiction to the very rules set up for it, just because they wanted to do something to keep the plot going. That's not playing fair with the audience. It has nothing to do with *Star Trek*; it has to do with telling a story. So then add to that the fact that it's supposed to be a reinvention of characters that you grew up emotionally invested in. And it felt like, well, this is not *Star Trek*."

The next of the Kelvin timeline films received a bit of a warmer welcome, as the storytelling at least was better (in my opinion). Still, some fans mockingly called it *Star Trek: Into Dumbness*. Some felt that the film borrowed too much from *Wrath of Kahn* (hint: it did) and that this was just a retelling with a twist, a different Kirk and Spock, but without the thirty years of friendship to back their actions up.

Others thought that Abram's take was a good thing, and while arguments continue over whether he was an actual fan of the series or more of a *Star Wars* guy, many think he at least liked the "Big Idea" of Trek. In the first film of the Kelvin timeline, he did a poor job of it, instead bringing in too many "Star Wars Magic" elements to the more science-focused (mostly) *Star Trek* world.

But with *Into Darkness*, the acclaimed director at least started to figure out that this was a different universe, and although he turned Kirk into an action hero, a Jason Bourne type but more vocal with a better social life (unlike Bourne, Kirk has friends), fans could almost see a young Captain Kirk of TOS somewhere in this character's future. Still, even in *Star Trek Beyond*, we see a young Federation, not one of eager young explorers but of soldiers shooting their way through the galaxy, and many fans wondered if the original premise of peaceful exploration was one that would never be revisited again.

That film suffered from a lot of pre-production issues, and the script was rewritten several times because the original draft was horrible. It ended with a promise of a new voyage for the Kelvin timeline, a new and rebuilt *USS Enterprise*, and more adventures with this young crew to come, and just announced during the revision of this book, a fourth film in this series is in development.

Overall, the new Kirk is young, brash, and inexperienced. He'll break the rules to achieve the mission or to save lives, and by the (current) end of the Kelvin timeline series, he more closely resembles the Kirk fans of TOS know and love. However, for true fans of TOS, there are some differences. To really enjoy the films, we just must acknowledge that this is a different work entirely, but one that uses some elements that were part of the original.

While the casting and the acting for the young version of Scotty and McCoy also solidify by the third film, the portrayal of Mr. Spock is--odd. One could say even illogical. This has polarized Trekkies for a variety of reasons. The new version of Spock is more in touch with his humanity. When he suffers the loss of his world (the destruction of Vulcan) and then loses his father during this series, we see an emotional, even illogical reaction. He does not always follow logic and even works to seek revenge (*Into the Darkness*).

With the final of the initial Kelvin timeline films complete, the current period of *Star Trek* films and series began.

THE EXPANSION OF THE *STAR TREK* UNIVERSE (2016-PRESENT)

Initially, in the mid-2000s, CBS turned down several offers, including from Jonathan Frakes and William Shatner, to bring the series back to the small screen. And in reality, the films were dominating the small screen already, along with the series that already existed. Thanks to streaming services like Netflix and Amazon Prime, the shows became available to more people than ever before, at least temporarily.

To capitalize on this trend, CBS did a few key things. First, they launched *Star Trek Discovery*, a new live-action series that premiered in September of 2017. The second season premiered in January 2019, the third season in late 2020, and the fourth season is airing during the writing of this book (more on that in a later chapter).

How did hardcore fans react? Well, again, fans were polarized. Some loved the new direction, the more political intrigue rather than a constant battle. Most of the positive reactions showed fans appreciated the nods to the series that had come before, but the real bonus is the attraction of a new and younger set of fans who aren't hanging on to the same nostalgia as some of us lifelong Trekkies.

Other fans hated the show (including a Facebook commenter two days before the writing of this chapter). The cinematography is different, more modern, there is a lot of bickering among crew members at least initially, and the Klingons—we don't talk about the Klingons.

Then there were a few fans who were kind of middle of the road. They wanted the new series to be its own thing, not just a part of the previous universe. They thought it was okay, but they were also not overly enthusiastic.

Personally, I (Troy) fell into the first camp, with some of the same feelings as the middle of the road camp. I think the series should be taken as its own thing, I like the new take on the Trek universe, and I don't mind new cinematography and the move toward political intrigue. I'm a little "Trek Battle Weary" and sometimes wish we were closer to the TOS Prime Directive.

All this is to be expected. Jonathan Frakes compared the reaction of fans to TNG when it first aired, and to be fair, the first season of TNG was not great or heartwarmingly embraced by fans either, until the series found its legs in season two. "I don't think it wasn't until the second or third year when the show really got good," that fans started to accept TNG, as Frakes recalls in an interview with Galaxy Con Live. "And remember we did 26 [episodes] a year, so that is a lot. It was 50, 60 shows in. They realized there was room in their worlds for both shows."

And in a recent rewatch of TNG Season 1, I can't help but agree. It took me a minute to warm up to it, and looking back, in the future I may just skip season one and kind of pretend it didn't happen, but that Picard was always the great, beloved captain and example of leadership he became.

The truth about pleasing Trekkies seems to be more complicated than one might suppose. Fans of TOS want to see more Spock, McCoy, and Kirk the way they remember them. Nostalgia and familiarity lead to less openness to new series and new takes on *The Tao of Trek*. Those who accepted and loved *TNG* want to see more Picard-like stories and more content in that timeline.

There are those (including me) who want *Star Trek* to get back to its roots--a show about exploration, not space battles, war, and hand-to-hand combat. Less military sci-fi and more human stories. That's what drew me to the series in the first place.

And that is what happened with the release of *Star Trek Picard*, which premiered on January 23, 2020. The series brought TNG fans back into the world of an older Picard set on a new adventure, and a second season is airing during this writing. The show is beloved because of its direct connection to both a beloved *Star Trek* series and a favorite central character.

Currently, there are plans to create several series in the *Star Trek* universe. All of them are tied to the streaming service Paramount +, and many consider that tie as a source of its success. Partnerships with both Netflix (*Discovery*) and Amazon Prime (*Picard*) give those streaming services the rights to stream the series internationally. The series of shorts, called *Star Trek: Short Treks*, offers standalone mini episodes that air between *Discovery* and *Picard* Seasons, designed to keep fans engaged.

And there's more. Alex Kurtzman signed a five-year deal with CBS to expand the series and has plans that go out to 2027, citing the length it takes to produce each show. An additional streaming series, *Strange New Worlds*, was announced in May of 2020 and is currently set for release, although to the chagrin of many fans, as of this writing, there is no trailer.

A new animated series, which we will address in more detail later, *Lower Decks*, has also emerged. It is an adult-style cartoon sharing a producer with the Adult Swim *Rick and Morty*. It too, is not an unequivocal hit with Trekkies. Some love it; some hate it. A less adult animation, *Star Trek: Prodigy*, is airing on Paramount + (produced in conjunction with Nickelodeon), and frankly, it is one of my favorite animated Trek shows so far (go watch it).

What does all this mean for *The Tao of Trek*? Well, quite simply, as society and television evolve, so does the show and the philosophy behind it. The controversial Kelvin timeline shows polarized fans for that reason: TOS and even TNG were shows about peaceful exploration and the conflict that arises from that mission. *DS9* showed us what it was like to try to maintain that peace at a remote outpost during a period of war. *Voyager* continued that theme. We won't talk about *Enterprise* and its failings, at least not yet.

But in the rebooted JJ Abrams world, there was a lot more space fantasy and a lot more military sci-fi-like direct conflict: the action/adventure aspect drew new fans, those for whom Michael Bay level lens flares and sweeping camera angles define space cinema.

What about the future? *Strange New Worlds* seems to embrace a more exploration-based theme, but time will tell. *Lower Decks* is a humorous but very human look, at the lesser known but equally important members of every crew.

One thing is sure. We're going to see more *Picard*, and I can't wait. We will likely see more *Discovery*. And we can hope that out of all of these; new Trekkies are born, those who can respect the heritage of the original shows yet find ways to embrace the latest versions of them. And perhaps, if we are all lucky, some will grow up to write and produce more *Star Trek* adventures - and maybe, just maybe, those values will translate to the world we live in as well.

For that is the goal of *The Tao of Trek*. We want to go beyond entertainment. We want to examine the things Trek has to teach us, and then we want to apply them to our lives, our society, and the way we deal with each other as we stand on the precipice of the reality of traveling to, exploring, and even living beyond our home planet.

In that light, let's look at the "when" behind the *Star Trek* universe. Where, and how, does all this fit into some kind of timeline?

Before we can truly answer that question though, we must first look at where that timeline comes from. What series and books actually establish that timeline? What is part of *Star Trek*'s official canon, and what isn't?

CHAPTER 2
THE CHANGING DEFINITION
OF CANON

~

Okay, so a note before we get started down the road of *Star Trek* history: we must establish, or at least clarify, the official Star Trek canon issue. You will often hear films, books, and other things as "canon" or "non-canon". The question of what we mean by that is a bit more complicated than it initially seems, especially when we add what I am going to call the Gene Roddenberry (GR) Factor.

First, some purists would say that only GR-approved series and films where he was involved in the creation or production process are considered canon. However, that would remove seven films (to date) from canon and all the series that came after his death. Because this defies Roddenberry himself and his desire for the series to go on, for the sake of *Tao of Trek*, we won't take that view of what is canon.

From there, things can get even trickier because Gene Roddenberry himself was somewhat of a revisionist. Just because he considered something to be canon at one point doesn't mean he always thought that way. In fact, he often changed his mind later on, as Paula Bok shared when talking about her conversations with him in 2005:

"Another thing that makes canon a little confusing. Gene R. himself had a habit of de-canonizing things. He didn't like the way the animated series turned out, so he proclaimed that it was not canon. He also didn't like a lot of the movies. So, he didn't much consider them canon either. And – okay, I'm really going to scare you with this one – after he got TNG [*Star Trek: The Next Generation*] going, he... well... he sort of decided that some of The Original Series wasn't canon either. I had a discussion with him once, where I cited a couple of things that were very clearly canon in The Original Series (TOS), and he told me he didn't think that way anymore, and that he now thought of TNG as canon wherever there was a conflict between the two. He admitted it was revisionist thinking, but so be it."

Because of Rodenberry himself, The Animated Series (TAS) was not considered canon for two decades before it was accepted canon by most *Star Trek* fans. Also, writers drew from works not considered to be canon for works inside the canon. This is true of the first names of Hikaru Sulu and Nyota Uhura, both first used in the non-canonical book *The Entropy Effect*, which I vividly remember reading with much delight.

Kirk's middle name, Tiberius, also came from TAS, first used in canon in *Star Trek VI: The Undiscovered Country*. Other examples of this type of non-canon material being adopted into canon are plentiful.

As to films, all the original series films are considered canon, as are extra deleted scenes included in director's cut versions. However, the "extra features" on DVDs have not been addressed adequately enough to call them canon or non-canon. To add to the confusion, Roddenberry himself did not like some of the films as stated above but really didn't specify, for instance, what he didn't like about them, and what parts he did not consider to be part of the canon.

When it comes to books, comics, and novelizations of episodes, none of these are considered canon. The only exceptions are the non-fiction guides: *The Star Trek Encyclopedia, Star Trek Chronology, Star Trek: The Next Generation Technical Manual,* and *Star Trek: Deep Space Nine Technical Manual.* Roddenberry considered them "Trek background", but they were sanctioned by Paramount and given to episode writers to use for reference, bringing them into canon by association.

There are exceptions to the book rule, but they are few and far between. In fact, this book you are reading is clearly not canon, as it is a fan work of nonfiction. To the best of our ability, it is designed to be transformative and point to the original works as faithfully as possible but is not sanctioned by Paramount, nor should it be considered canon in the same way that many fan works of fiction are not.

So perhaps this next paragraph should be taken with a grain of salt, but when it comes to *The Tao of Trek,* we will consider the canon to be that followed at startrek.com, but with a caveat. Just because something is not canon does not mean we won't include it in our timeline or talk about it. After all, *The Tao of Trek* is primarily lived and shaped by the fans, so things like fan films, fan fiction, and even unofficial book spin-offs should be treated as part of what makes up the overall philosophy of the Tao.

However, for the sake of clarity, according to the *Star Trek* database linked above (or contained on startrek.com if you are reading a physical version of this book rather than an eBook), the following series are considered canon (and likely others will be added as they become available)

- *The Original Series (TOS)*
- *The Animated Series (TAS)*

- *The Next Generation (TNG)*
- *Deep Space 9 (DS9)*
- *Voyager (VOY)*
- *Enterprise (ENT)*
- *Picard (PIC)*
- *Discovery (DIS)*
- *Lower Decks (LW)*
- *Short Treks (ST)*
- *Prodigy (PRO)*
- *Strange New Worlds (SNW)*

Note that we include anything popularly considered canon, whether we like it or not. This includes films included in the canon as well:

- *Star Trek The Motion Picture*
- *Wrath of Kahn*
- *Search for Spock*
- *The Voyage Home*
- *The Final Frontier*
- *Undiscovered Country*
- *Generations*
- *Insurrection*
- *First Contact*
- *Nemesis*
- *Star Trek* (2009)
- *Into Darkness*
- *Beyond*
- *The Next Kelvin Timeline Film*

As with other works, we don't include fan-created films, even ill-fated ones killed by Paramount, but that likely would have been great additions to the franchise. We could have included the script of that show, but to do so would potentially change the purity of the Tao. (We will discuss that in more detail later, though).

Fan works are often at the heart of Trek philosophy, and they have great value. Although we can't adopt them into any "official" canon, we can acknowledge and respect them.

CLASSIC CANON VS. THE KELVIN TIMELINE

We're not going to go in too deep here, but when Star Trek rebooted in 2009, there was a bit of a debate. How do you reboot a franchise whose fans are, shall we say, passionate about canon? Well, you really have two choices. Either stick with the series with over 50 years of television history and find yourself really limited in what you can and cannot do, or…

Throw in some time travel and create an alternate timeline that lets the "new" series continue without directly contradicting the original films and canon. Essentially, when trying to save Romulus from being destroyed by a supernova in 2387, Spock and a Romulan mining ship are hurled back in time, emerging at different years. We won't post spoilers here (go watch the films for yourself), but we will say that this causes Starfleet to shift their focus. They still want to seek out new life forms, but it's no longer an entirely peaceful exploration. They need to find out how dangerous these new life forms are and whether they will become allies of the Federation or enemies.

The second film in the timeline is a revised retelling of the *Wrath of Kahn* but ends with then Enterprise being assigned its five-year mission. There has been some crossover with the prime timeline, most specifically in *Picard*. Again, no spoilers here, but it is safe to say that we may see films or shows set in either the Kelvin timeline or the crossover timelines, as long as the writers are cautious about not violating either the established canon that started with TOS or the "new" canon set in motion by Kelvin.

In short, our canon lines up with the official canon of Star Trek, and this allows room for argument about whether or not it aligns with the ideas of GR, the principles of the Tao, or if it is just an officially licensed property of the Trek franchise that should be included in any analysis.

Now that we know where the timeline of the franchise comes from, at least as far as canon is defined at the moment, we can look at the "series timeline" in some detail and define how it relates to the evolution of *The Tao of Trek*.

CHAPTER 3
STARDATE WHAT? THE SERIES TIMELINE

The internal chronology of Star Trek is always up for debate, what with time travel, time loops, timelines, prequels, sequels, crossovers, and do-overs. Who knows if it is Tuesday or your elbow? And it doesn't help that the basic idea of the Stardate doesn't actually line up with real-time, even internally. Many of the series used different methods of calculating the Stardate. The Original Series writers were instructed to pick any combination of four numbers plus a single number after the decimal point to use as the starting point for their episode. Additional dates should progress logically in that script but didn't need to line up with other scripts. So, each episode had its own internal calendar, which didn't match the rest of the episodes.

By the time of The Next Generation, Stardates expanded to five digits with additional numbers after the decimal. The rules were a bit more rigid, with the first digit representing the century and the second the show's season. The first season used 41 as their leading digits, and the final three digits progressed from 000 to 999 throughout the season. The numbers after the decimal were adjusted from days to fractions of a day as the series continued.

But none of these systems were followed consistently without fail, so there are exceptions everywhere. I'll try and keep things in order and give you some idea of when they are happening, but don't count on it being perfectly accurate since even the writers of the show can't agree!

Let's kick off the timeline with the earliest date recorded, which just happens to be the earliest date possible:

The Big Bang! | ST: Voyager | Time Travel

The birth of the Universe. That's right; Star Trek went where no one had gone before, the birth of the universe. That was in the second season of Voyager in the episode "Death Wish". This is the earliest Stardate by well over 13 billion years, a record which will probably stay unbroken no matter how many other time travel episodes are created.

5,000 years in the past | ST: TOS | Time Travel

On the planet Sarpeidon. During the second to last episode of The Original Series, "All Our Yesterdays", Spock and McCoy are sent through a time travel device known as the Atavachron into the planet's ice age. They are able to return, but an interesting aspect of the trip involves Spock reverting to the less logical mindset of the Vulcans of that time.

17th Century | ST: TOS | Time Travel

On Earth! In merry old England to be exact. Kirk is separated from Spock and McCoy in the same episode, "All Our Yesterdays", and tried as a witch for his ability to still hear his friends in the other time.

Spock's Childhood | ST: TAS | Time Travel/Alternate

On Vulcan, but with no specific date. In The Animated Series' second episode, "Yesteryear", research with the Guardian of Forever (first shown in The Original Series "City on the Edge of

Forever") causes Spock's history to be cut short and him to loop back and save himself from dying as a child.

1930 | ST: TOS | Time Travel

Earth during the Great Depression. This is the crew's first encounter with the Guardian of Forever, a time portal on an empty planet, where McCoy accidentally travels back to 1930, and Kirk and Spock must follow in order to bring him back.

1944 | ST: Enterprise | Time Travel/Alternate

An alternate Earth where the Nazis are winning World War II. Enterprise episode "Storm Front" pits the Enterprise and crew against time-traveling aliens and the Nazi war machine.

1968 | ST: TOS | Time Travel

Earth once again. This is one of two episodes where the Enterprise travels back to a time that overlaps the actual time the show is being produced. In "Assignment: Earth", they travel to conduct historical research but encounter an agent from another world who is there to interfere with Earth's history.

1969 | ST: TOS | Time Travel

Earth. In "Tomorrow is Yesterday", the Enterprise accidentally travels back and interferes with history, leading to them working with an Air Force pilot to correct the changes before returning to their own time.

1986 | ST IV: The Voyage Home | Time Travel

Earth, San Francisco. The last time the original cast traveled back in time was Star Trek IV: The Voyage Home. In order to save the present, they must travel back to the past and steal a whale. Yes, a whale. It's amazing how strange some plots sound when you cut them down to one sentence.

1992-1996 | ST: TOS and II: The Wrath of Khan | Milestone

Earth. This milestone is a controversial historic event, the Eugenics Wars. In The Original Series episode "Space Seed" (as well as *Star Trek II: The Wrath of Khan*), the genetically engineered "superman" Khan Noonien Singh comes from this time, having been frozen and exiled from Earth in the ship *SS Botany Bay* only to be awakened about 200 years later by the crew of the Enterprise. During the Eugenics Wars, Khan's forces conquered over a third of the planet, and millions of people died.

1996 | ST: Voyager | Time Travel

Earth. This episode involves time travel again, but here's where the controversy starts. In the Voyager episode "Future's End", the ship is pulled into the past and arrives in Earth's past. It's 1996, but no one mentions a war. A traveler from the 29th century visits the 24th century but pulls Voyager back to the 20th century. They must all work to restore history and return to their own times without causing any more damage. Some books have tried to straighten out what happened to the Eugenics Wars, while comic series covered their events, and other episodes moved the dates around. We may never know exactly what happened in Star Trek's timeline, but thankfully we've been spared this conflict in our own (so far!).

2063 | ST: First Contact | Time Travel

Earth, time travel courtesy of The Next Generation and the Borg. The Enterprise-E travels back to prevent the Borg from interfering in history, specifically the first flight of the warp drive and the first contact of Humans with Vulcans, as portrayed in *Star Trek: First Contact*.

At last we've reached the era of the actual shows! While time travel still occurs, more of it is from this time to another rather than back to this time… with some exceptions.

2151-2155 | Star Trek: Enterprise | Series

This prequel to the original series explored the time before the Federation began. Although events from 900 years in the future came back to impact it.

2161 | ST: Enterprise | Milestone

The United Federation of Planets began in this year, pulling together Humans, Vulcans, Andoians, and other races.

2164 | ST: Beyond | Milestone

Shortly after the Federation is founded, the starship *USS Franklin*, seen in ST: Beyond, disappears.

2233 | Star Trek (2009) | Time Travel/Milestone

Nero, the Romulan captain, travels back in time from 2387, where he destroys the *USS Kelvin* and begins the Kelvin Timeline.

2254 | ST: TOS | Pilot

The very first Star Trek, the pilot episode "The Cage", which was rejected by NBC. Later in The Original Series, this episode was used to create a two-part episode, "The Menagerie", by being intercut with new footage of the new crew. The older footage is described as being from 13 years prior in the episode.

2255-2259 | Star Trek: Discovery | Series

Still set before The Original Series, *Discovery* introduces new characters and new technologies on the *USS Discovery*. *Discovery* engages in time travel as well, but in an effort to prevent some of the other issues with the prequels, the crew travels far into the future, and that is really where the show takes place. For some fans, this has created debate about the technology in the show and why it (at least at times) seems more advanced than technology in TOS.

2258 | Star Trek (2009) | Film/Alternate

Story of the Enterprise in an alternate timeline (popularly known as the Kelvin Timeline). This alternate is based on a future event, the destruction of Romulus, and a renegade ship returning to 2233 to attempt to punish the Federation for their failure to save the planet. The impact of this changes the lives of the characters originally featured in The Original Series, allowing a reboot of the series without conflicting with existing canon.

2259-2260 | ST: Into Darkness | Film/Alternate

A continuation of the Kelvin Timeline recounting the story of Khan Noonien Singh. Elements from the movie ST II: The Wrath of Khan are introduced throughout with twists and reversals to create a new story but resonate strongly with fans of the original, generating, shall we say, mixed opinions.

2262 | ST: Beyond | Film/Alternate

The latest Kelvin Timeline story involves a highly advanced Star Base, a trip into a dangerous sector of space, the destruction of the Enterprise and the capture of her crew, and the discovery of a long-lost starship.

2265-2269 | Star Trek: The Original Series | Series

Planned as a 'five-year mission' but canceled after only three seasons; this is the starting point for the Star Trek franchise. Featuring stand-alone episodes rather than season-long arcs, it developed the major characters but introduced some recurring minor characters and many others who appeared for only a single episode.

2269-2270 | Star Trek: The Animated Series | Series

An animated continuation of The Original Series featuring the same main characters in further adventures. While its status has been debated over time, it is now officially considered canon.

2273 | ST: The Motion Picture | Film

The first of the films based on Star Trek, it featured most of the major characters with a few additions. Due to difficulties with its production, it was not the strong start to a new line of films fans had hoped for.

2285 | ST II: The Wrath of Khan | Film

Long considered the best of the Star Trek Films, it reintroduced Khan from The Original Series episode "Space Seed". It also became the template for the later Kelvin Timeline film, *Into Darkness*.

2285 | ST III: The Search for Spock | Film

Closely linked with the previous film, it continues the arc of Spock's sacrifice, integrating it with the Genesis device.

2286 | ST IV: The Voyage Home | Film/Time Travel

Following closely on the heels of the previous film, this finishes the character arc begun in The Wrath of Khan while introducing a new time-traveling adventure heading back to 1986 to steal a whale.

2287 | ST V: The Final Frontier | Film

While a previous film searched for Spock, this film searches for God. Spock's half-brother becomes a prophet and seeks out God in the center of the galaxy, using various machinations to have the Enterprise take him there.

2293 | ST VI: The Undiscovered Country | Film

The final film set only in the prime universe's Original Series timeline; it deals with the Klingon Empire joining the Federation.

2293 & 2371 | ST: Generations | Film/Time Travel

In this film, the crews of The Original Series and The Next Generation are both involved in stopping a planetary system from being destroyed in order to open something called the

Nexus. While not exactly time travel, the film does have both Kirk and Picard working together, despite an 80-year separation in time.

2364-2370 | Star Trek: The Next Generation | Series

The major resurgence of Trek on TV came with *The Next Generation*. With a new crew and even a new *Enterprise*, TNG took us into new adventures, both episodic and longer arcs, for many years.

2366 | ST: Prodigy | Time Travel/Milestone

The Diviner arrives in the past (Star Trek: Prodigy), which is effectively the inciting incident for this story, launching the adventures of Dal, Rok-Tahk, Jankom Pog, and even a holographic version of Janeway.

2369-2375 | Star Trek: Deep Space Nine | Series

Deep Space Nine concentrated on a space station and the travelers passing through it. The station is perched beside a wormhole leading from our Alpha Quadrant to the Gamma Quadrant far across the galaxy. Later in the series, a starship, *USS Defiant*, restored some of the travel stories to the plots. The later seasons formed the large story arc of the war between the Federation and the Dominion from the Gamma Quadrant.

2371-2378 | Star Trek: Voyager | Series

Returning to a more exploration-driven concept, this series followed the *USS Voyager* on its adventures in the Delta Quadrant, where it was unwillingly pulled to. The series follows their struggle to return to Federation space and the problems they encounter on the way.

2373 | ST: First Contact | Film/Time Travel

The first of The Next Generation films still involves time travel, but skipping The Original Series era, it returns to the time of the first successful warp drive flight. This travel is to prevent the Borg from traveling back and conquering the earth in the past.

2375 | ST: Insurrection, | Film

This film deals with a conspiracy within Starfleet attempting to steal a planet from its native inhabitants for its life-extending properties. The Enterprise disobeys orders to intervene.

2379 | ST: Nemesis | Film

This is the final film of The Next Generation cast, featuring a clone of Picard taking over the Romulan Empire in a coup. The Enterprise and crew protect the Federation from the Romulans. An interesting milestone is Janeway's promotion to Admiral and giving orders to Picard.

2380 | Star Trek: Lower Decks | Series

Lower Decks presents a major change to the usual concepts of Star Trek. Instead of first contact missions, they provide second contact, a lower-stress diplomatic mission. Also, the main characters are all of lower ranks rather than captains and first officers. Finally, this is the first return to animation rather than live-action episodes since TAS in the 1970s. But despite the emphasis on humor, the Tao is still strongly present.

2383 | Star Trek: Prodigy | Series

Another change to the Star Trek formula, Prodigy, introduces untrained crew who find a starship rather than being assigned to it. While it's possible to dismiss this as 'Star Trek Babies', it's actually a much deeper concept which will undoubtedly hold up over several seasons.

2399 | Star Trek: Picard | Series

Set twenty years after Nemesis, this series focuses on Picard and his sorrow over the events in his past. Retired from Starfleet and living on his family's vineyard, he encounters

Data's daughter and is drawn into the conflict for 'synth' rights.

2433 | ST: Prodigy | Time Travel/Milestone

Diviner travels back to the past (Star Trek: Prodigy). Also, roughly the time when The Federation makes first contact with the Vau N'Akat on Solum.

2959 | ST: Discovery | Milestone

The point in the show where dilithium reserves have been exhausted, creating a new crisis for the Federation.

Between 3038 and 3088 | ST: Discovery | Milestone

The Burn, the disastrous galaxy-wide event in which all dilithium suddenly went inert, and every warp core exploded. This nearly led to the collapse of the United Federation of Planets and made dilithium an even more sought-after resource.

3188-3199 | ST: Discovery | Time Travel

Discovery arrives in the future. This kicks off the time travel portion of *Discovery* and sets the intersection of the rebuilding Federation and the old Federation ideals brought into the future by the USS Discovery.

Circa 33rd Century | Short Treks | Episode

Short Treks, "Calypso", also involves the *USS Discovery*, long after it has been abandoned. A human soldier wakes on the ship and befriends the AI that saved him.

CONCLUSION?

For now, this will end our discussion on the series timeline. If you want to dive deeper, there are many resources on websites like startrek.com, and you can debate the timeline and see lots of lively discussions on Reddit.

For this book, this chapter helps set a foundation for when the series happened, all the timeline events that intersect with "real-time" and where the different properties fit.

There is potentially enough information on specific episodes and the overall timeline for a book of its own. But rather than go down that road, we will instead look next at the cast that made up the show, those who have written and sung about the show, and the cons that have been spawned by Trek before we dive into philosophy behind the series headfirst.

CHAPTER 4
THE CAST

We can't talk about Trek without also talking about actors on the series who went on to find success, even if Trek might have been their "big break." There are some obvious ones, some less obvious, and some who went on to be downright icons.

There are undoubtedly some we will miss here as well. To make a cohesive list might take a book all its own. So, we have taken a few we consider to be quite notable: actors who have gone on to be in other shows that have greatly influenced our culture.

Then we'll talk briefly about some downright icons. Many of them have books of their own about Trek, their careers, and more, and we encourage you to read those as well. After all, to include all that information and their memories would require a library of our own.

THE A-LIST

There are plenty of faces to recognize in Trek: **Scott Bakula** was quite well known before he joined *Enterprise* and took on the role of Captain in that series. He's had quite an acting career from time travel (*Quantum Leap*) to NCIS to the big screen and even directing roles. And to non-Trek fans, he may be best known for some of those roles.

Kirstie Alley was perhaps best known for her role as Rebecca on *Cheers* but also has appeared in countless television shows and films. A talented actress, she's played a variety of characters and has appeared in other shows that have become nearly as iconic. However, her role in *Wrath of Kahn* likely gave her career a significant boost from a film that remains a Trek fan favorite.

And we would be remiss not to mention **Jeffrey Combs**, who appeared in *DS9*, *Enterprise*, has now returned to Trek as part of *Lower Decks* but has since appeared all over the Hollywood map. He's been in *The 4400*, Justice League, *Chaddom*, and is a voice actor in many superhero and sci-fi animated series. His career spans decades beyond Trek, and he's made a significant impact wherever he's landed.

- **Andrew Robinson** was in *Hellraiser, Child's Play,* and even played the killer in *Dirty Harry* (1971).
- **Jeri Ryan** appeared in roles in Leverage, Bosch, Boston Public, the O.C., and Law and Order, and then returned to be a part of the cast in *Star Trek: Picard.*
- **Wil Wheaton** appeared in *Stand by Me* (the film adaptation of Stephen King's *The Body*), numerous other television shows, including appearing as himself on *Big Bang Theory.*
- **Alexander Siddig** appeared in *Game of Thrones.*
- **Colm Meany** went on to many significant roles (although his role in *Under Siege* was a stretch perhaps).
- **Kate Mulgrew (Captain Janeway)** has returned to Trek with an animated role in Prodigy, but perhaps her most well-known non-Trek role came in *Orange Is the New Black.*
- **LeVar Burton** did *Reading Rainbow* concurrently with his role on *TNG* and continues to be involved in that and

other programming for children. There was even talk of a potential stint as a *Jeopardy* host (although that did not pan out).

- **Whoopi Goldberg (Guinan)** is another great example. Nichelle Nichols was the first black woman Whoopi saw on television who wasn't a maid. This inspired her to become an actress. When she heard about *TNG*, she reached out to the showrunners because she wanted to contribute to *Star Trek* because of what it had meant to her.
- **Aron Eisenberg (Nog)** was very close to the fans of *Star Trek* and made regular posts and comments in a popular Trek Facebook group. He worked on a podcast reviewing all the episodes of *DS9* before he died in his 50s. As a result of his work, a ship was named after him in *Discovery* (the *Eisenberg*).
- **Avery Brooks (Sisko)** was the first black *Star Trek* captain, but he was one of the first representations of a good black father on television. He's had a prolific acting history, including personal favorites *Spenser for Hire* and the spinoff *A Man Called Hawk*. He's also musically talented, including his own album of jazz covers (and the spoken word) titled *Here*.
- **Cirroc Lofton (Jake Sisko)** hosted the podcast about *DS9* with Aron Eisenberg and continued the podcast after his co-host's passing. He played a professional basketball star in Showtime's *The Hoop Life* and *Soul Food*.
- **Garrett Wang** got his big break as Ensign Harry Kim, on *VOY*, and has since starred in the mini-series *Into the West* and in the fan production *Star Trek: Of Gods and Men*.
- **Robert Duncan McNeill** (Lieutenant Tom Paris *VOY*) not only acted but directed several episodes of *VOY* and many sci-fi and other shows, such as fan favorites like *Resident Alien*.

- **Anthony Rapp** and **Wilson Cruz** shared the first gay kiss on *Star Trek* (*DSC*). Anthony is a Broadway actor who played in *Rent, Charlie Brown,* and *If/Then* prior to his role on *Discovery*. Cruz played Rickie Vasquez on *My So-Called Life*, Angel in the Broadway tour production of *Rent*, and has a recurring role on *Noah's Arc* in addition to his role on *Discovery*.
- **Emily Coutts** and **Mary Chieffo** both came out as LGBTQ+ in part because of the amazing representation of LGBTQ+ folks on *Discovery*. Coutts has starred in and directed several short indie films before her Trek debut (and continues to do so). Chieffo has also appeared in several short films, including the animated short *On the Day You Were Born* prior to her Klingon role on *Discovery*.
- **Ian Alexander** and **Blu del Barrio** are the first trans/non-binary characters on Trek. Alexander is an actor and writer known for *The Last of Us Part II* and *The OA*. Del Barrio acted in theater and several short films before joining the cast of *Discovery* in 2020.
- **Mathilde O'Callaghan "Tig" Notaro** (Chief Engineer Jett Reno) has an impressive stand-up and comedy career, including her Emmy award-winning *Tig Notaro: Boyish Girl Interrupted* and Grammy-nominated comedy album *Live*.

T hat leaves us with some pretty iconic stars who either got their break or just had extensive careers related to Trek. But many went beyond those roles: far beyond.

A HANDFUL OF ICONS

There are some obvious Trek icons. They are the ones who everyone lines up to meet at cons until they either can't do those cons anymore, or like many of our favorites, have passed on to explore the world of the afterlife, a place far beyond our knowledge.

Here is a look at a few of them and what they have meant to us.

James Montgomery Doohan (Mr. Scott) | March 3, 1920-July 20, 2005)

Known to all of us "old Trekkies" quite simply as Scotty, Doohan never did really take off in other roles. However, he did do an incredible amount for *Star Trek*, appearing at conventions, voicing his character in TAS, and appearing on the big screen in the various Trek films as well.

His real claim to fame? The often-misquoted phrase, "Beam me up, Scotty!" This appears on bumper stickers, t-shirts, and has become a part of cultures everywhere, signaling the desire to be transported out of a variety of situations.

Walter Koenig (Mr. Chekov)

One of the few surviving cast members of TOS, Koenig not only played the role of Pavel Chekov in TOS, but also did multiple voices in TAS, played his role in all the original cast *Star Trek* films, is another con favorite, and has appeared on Babylon 5, authored comics and books, and had a significant influence on both Trekkies and society as a whole.

DeForest Kelley (Dr. McCoy) | January 20, 1920-June 11, 1999

Much like James Doohan, perhaps DeForest Kelley is most remembered for things he said on *Star Trek*. Two catchphrases have made their way in to mainstream references:

- "I'm a doctor, Jim, not a magician!" and
- "It's worse than that. He's dead, Jim."

Both have morphed to include a variety of references, including many occupational substitutions for "doctor." (How do I say "I'm an author, not a mathematician" to the IRS in a professional email? Asking for a friend.) Add to that all the phrases substituting "he's dead" for "it's dead, Jim" referring to all manner of things, and the impact of the character of Dr. McCoy and the man who played him can't be contained in any one paragraph.

But Kelley was also an extremely popular actor in Westerns before Trek, including appearances in *Gunfight at the O.K. Corral* (as Morgan Earp); *Warlock* (with Henry Fonda); and several television shows. He often played villains, and to break the potential typecast, he appeared in *Where Love Has Gone*. He also played in two pilots that never made it into series production: *333 Montgomery* and *Police Story*, both created by Gene Roddenberry.

For many of us, his death signaled the end of an era. He was the first of the Original Series cast to pass away, the only one in the 1900s. Besides TOS, he also appeared as an admiral in the first episode of TNG. His passing reminded us that our Trek heroes were far from eternal, just like the rest of us.

There are those cast members still among us who continue to inspire, but Dr. McCoy will, in a way, always be with us.

Brent Spiner (Data)

Brent Spiner is not only an actor but a comedian best known for his role as the android Data in TNG. But his career was about more than that. Initially, he too started out in the theater, starring in several on and off-Broadway shows, and earning a variety of film credits before joining TNG in 1987.

After Trek, Spiner continued an amazing acting career. He's appeared in episodes of several popular shows, from *Blacklist* and *Law and Order* to *South Park* and other comedies. He's also a fan favorite at cons, and loves to talk to and interact with Trekkies. He's a voice and an advocate for *Star Trek: Fleet Command* and a handful of other Star Trek games as well. He, like Data, has truly become an icon in the eyes of fans the world over.

Jonathan Frakes (Riker)

There are those Trekkies who are solidly divided over whether they like the character of Riker or not, but there can be no doubt about his influence in the past and his continuing influence on Trek. He's not only acted in multiple series, including *Picard* but he's also directed multiple episodes as well, some of them iconic in nature.

They include the films *First Contact* and *Insurrection*, TNG episodes "Reunion", "Cause and Effect", and "The Chase", along with two episodes of *Picard*. But his reach goes far beyond what he has done with Trek to shows like *Leverage, Burn Notice, NCIS, The Librarians*, and more.

And there is no doubt that Frakes will continue to influence Trek in a big way.

Patrick Stewart (Captain Jean-Luc Picard)

We're working our way, in no particular order, to some of the icons of Trek that have been in our lives and hearts for years but who have transcended their television roles to have grand ones elsewhere.

Patrick Stewart had a difficult task as Captain Picard. He had to, in the hearts and minds of "Old Trek" fans of the time, somehow equal Captain Kirk to be a "real leader" in Starfleet. And as discussed previously, Season 1 of TNG certainly did not make that easy. But things got better, and thankfully so until Picard became loved in his own right.

Leadership books have been written (*Make it So*, by Wess Roberts is the most popular) from the leadership style and actions of the beloved captain. And many, reportedly even Roddenberry at one point, came to believe he was a better captain than Kirk, or at least his equal.

In fact, the debate over who was better still rages and fuels fan memes everywhere. This has been tainted somewhat by the return of Stewart in *Picard*. Some love the new series and the new show, and like all takes on Trek, others still hate it.

Personally, we like the show for what it is. There are moments when we see characters from past shows pass, or we get a glimpse of the Trek as it used to be, that it even makes us sad. From all reports, Season 3 will be filled with more of the same.

No matter what your take, though, it is clear the impact Stewart has had on just this series. When you add his contributions to X-Men and other franchises, it is clear he has become an icon indeed.

George Takei (Mr. Sulu)

Not only is George Takei our "Sulu" but he is so much more. He brought incredible life and acting skills to TOS, but he did more than that. He began to represent marginalized groups in a big way.

Not only does Takei represent and advocate for the LGBTQ+ community as a gay man married to the love of his life (Brad, who we would love to meet if you are reading this George), but he also represents Japanese Americans who were imprisoned in the United States during World War II.

He's written and performed in a musical, *Allegiance*, which talks about this very topic. His family was imprisoned even though they had been in the United States for some time, and he talks about his perception of those events, even as a young boy. He's also written a book about the topic and continues to educate anyone who will listen about these often forgotten or ignored events.

And he shows no signs of slowing down. Besides that, Takei is funny and has embraced social media in a huge way. He's one of the funniest people to follow, and he often shares pearls of wisdom amongst that humor, a lesson we could all learn from.

Takei has become an icon that his role as Sulu is only a part of. He truly has gone "where no man has gone before" and set an example for us by also "going boldly." He truly embodies *The Tao of Trek*.

Marina Sirtis (Deanna Troi)

Marina Sirtis not only played Deanna Troi in several different Trek series but had a robust film and video game career as well. She trained classically in acting, starting her career in the theater. Once she had mastered her craft, she moved on to television and films. Before TNG, she appeared in several British television series.

Sirtis also appeared in films including *The Wicked Lady*, *Blind Date* (with **Kirstie Alley**), and *Death Wish 3*. Following TNG, she took on voice-over roles in the series Gargoyles, and has appeared since in several films, science fiction shows besides TNG, and several video games as well.

She's a shining example of acting prowess that not only improved TNG and made it better but propelled her to other fantastic roles. As a regular at cons, she's a fan favorite the world over.

Gates McFadden (Beverly Crusher)

Before TNG, Gates McFadden worked for Jim Henson Productions as a choreographer, and to keep her acting and choreography work separate; she often was credited as Cheryl

McFadden. She appeared on *The Cosby Show*, *When Nature Calls*, and briefly as the wife of Jack Ryan in *The Hunt for Red October*. Her role in TNG initially stopped after season one, when Maurice Hurley, the showrunner, didn't care for working with her. A new love interest for Picard, Dr. Katherine Pulaski, took her place for season 2. However, that character did not resonate well with fans, so for seasons 3-7, McFadden returned as Beverly Crusher.

After TNG, she went on to several film roles, including *Crowned and Dangerous* and *Taking Care of Business*, along with all the Next Generation films and several theater appearances. Also a fan favorite at cons, McFadden truly has become an icon for Trekkies everywhere.

Nichelle Nichols (Lt. Uhura)

The role of Lt. Uhura was only the start for Nichelle, who nearly quit the show but was reportedly encouraged by Dr. Martin Luther King to remain in the role. And remain she did. Nichols became an inspiration for a generation of women of color and was a part of one of the most iconic Trek moments on television, a kiss shared with William Shatner as James T. Kirk.

By the time I saw the episode in syndication, the hype had died down considerably, but at the time, such a thing was earth-shattering. But that was just the beginning. Not only was the cast of TOS diverse, but the whole principle of acceptance set the stage for something else: women in space.

NASA was long a bastion of white-malehood seeking the stars. While women and women of color were in the organization, they were hidden in segregated buildings. White men controlled what we saw, so we saw astronauts, those who would actually visit space.

The key to remember is that even NASA wanted to work with Nichols with one thing in mind: invite more women into the space program. It was because of this that Mae Jemison, an astronaut, appeared on an episode of *TNG*.

Little did they know how tenacious she would be, far beyond a consulting or advertising figure. She insisted on change and persisted until she saw it.

But Nichols never left Trek and her fans there far behind. Until recent years and a decline in both physical and mental health, Nichelle Nichols remained a fan favorite at cons around the world, and she always had time for fans.

She's an icon, an advocate, and a wonderful person we can all seek to emulate.

Troy: I've saved two icons for last, not because they are any greater than any of the others on this list, but because they both have inspired me in unique ways.

Leonard Nimoy (Mr. Spock) | March 26, 1931 – February 27, 2015

I almost can't write this section because although it has been seven years (as of this writing) since his passing, I cannot help but miss Leonard Nimoy, aka Mr. Spock.

He has not only done much to inspire *The Tao of Trek*, but his character both on and off-screen, taught us things about honesty, philosophy, and how we should live our lives. New actors are wonderful, and some do a great job in the films they are in, but Nimoy will forever be Mr. Spock to me.

I'll never forget the pain of the ending of *Wrath of Kahn* or the joy of *The Search for Spock*. Over the years, as I look back, nearly every time I think of a favorite quote from Trek, it came from Spock. Quite literally, the idea that logic might actually rule over emotion or at least improve it was all I needed to start looking at life in a different light.

And my life changed. I am sure others could express similar thoughts. For me, Spock was Trek, and I will forever miss Nimoy's brilliant portrayal of him.

William Shatner (Captain James T. Kirk)

What can I say about William "Bill" Shatner that has not been said? Not a damn thing. As of this writing, the man has just returned from an actual space flight, albeit a short one. He's an author, screenwriter, spokesperson, comedian, fan-favorite, but more importantly, for many, he is "us".

Captain Kirk, and Shatner, are flawed humans. His character is impulsive, brash, overly emotional, an occasional womanizer, and yet we love him. Why? Because we too are flawed. We try to live up to our own Prime Directives, and we fail (more on that later in the book). When we do what we think is right, it often isn't.

Sometimes that works out. Other times it does not. Much of the time, we will put ourselves last, willing to risk our own lives but not willing to let others risk theirs. We put our needs under others' and turn around and try to take control of situations beyond our control.

We worry. We obsess. We act rashly. And we pay the price. Shatner is no exception. There are things named after him. If your director wants you to "overact" a role, they will tell you to "Shatner" it. He's as good-natured in person as he is on the screen, yet he also has a serious side.

Trekkie or not, many in our culture at least know of "Captain Kirk" and Shatner himself, if not from Trek, than from one of his many other roles. He's the very definition of an icon.

Friendships, Frenemies, and More

Many of the stars of the various Trek series have found themselves at odds with one another. Most of the time, they end up working it out, and we won't go into great, tabloid-like detail here. We'll simply say that for many, they were living out *The Tao of Trek*: they are human, just as we all are. We have things that unite us and things that could potentially divide us.

But in the end, we're all here on this rock together, hurtling through space, seeking some kind of peace. We may not agree on how to get there, but we may agree that we, as humans, need to do better.

And from icons to actors, from writers to directors, from fans to superfans, the cast and followers of Trek have changed the world. We hope we have only changed it for the better and will continue to do so.

If we've missed true icons here that you think we should have included, please let us know. We'll keep adding to our website (and future editions of this book, I am sure), so we would love to hear from you.

Now, let's explore yet another group of Trekkies who have changed the world, the tribe of which we are members: the bards and minstrels of Trek.

CHAPTER 5
BARDS AND MINSTRELS

"The Romulans may rip this base in half, pal. They may even kill me. But I'll be damned if they're going to keep me from enjoying a refreshing beverage."

— Michael Jan Friedman, Starfleet Year One

"Saavik gazed calmly at the viewscreen. She was aesthetically elegant in the spare, understated, esoterically powerful manner of a Japanese brush painting."

— Vonda N. McIntyre, Star Trek II: The Wrath Of Khan

"Even in your world, people have died for words. Sometimes they've died of them. One learns to be careful what one says in such a world. And like anything so powerful, like any weapon, words cut both ways. They redeem and betray—sometimes both at once. The attribute we name as a virtue may also turn out to be our bane. So we watch what we call things—in case we should turn out to be right."

— Diane Duane, My Enemy, My Ally

"Despite centuries of English literature, the most famous split infinitive in all of history comes from Star Trek."

— *R. Curtis Venture*

∽

F irst of all, we can't talk about bards and minstrels without a salute to perhaps the greatest bard of all, William Shakespeare. The "original bard" had not only a great influence on Roddenberry and the Trek franchise but modern television and film as a whole.

Really, influence from Shakespeare's plays and poetry isn't something created by *Star Trek* or limited to it. The English language overflows with phrases popularized by Shakespeare, and our literature abounds with plots and situations used by the Bard. But *Star Trek* did use some of these elements with little or no changes, such as The Conscience of the King from the Original Series first season. In it, a Shakespearian theater troupe is suspected of concealing a genocidal leader. From the title to the many scenes of the actors performing, to the tragic plotline this episode reeks of Shakespeare.

I suppose this shouldn't surprise anyone who knows how many actors from the series performed in Shakespeare companies before being cast. William Shatner, Patrick Stewart, and Avery Brooks all trod the boards for the Bard. Christopher Plummer, the antagonist from *Star Trek VI: The Undiscovered Country* and a Shakespearean actor, quoted extensively from the plays during his performance. In addition to Commander Sisko on Deep Space Nine, many of the other actors had a close relationship to Shakespeare's plays, with Armin Shimerman performing and teaching the subject.

These actors brought their love of the theater into their characters, from Picard having a copy of *The Globe Illustrated Shakespeare* in his quarters (I have one on my shelf too!) as well as Data having a copy of the collected works. Quotes and themes from the Bard are used throughout the series to illustrate timeless insights into humanity and even alien species. Production staff also contributed by naming many Original Series episodes with quotes from Shakespeare. *All Our Yesterdays, By Any Other Name, The Conscience of the King, Dagger of the Mind,* and *The Undiscovered Country* are all taken from plays.

More comically, the final Original Series film spawned versions translated into Klingon containing the line "You don't know Shakespeare until you've heard it in the original Klingon." *The Klingon Hamlet* and a Klingon version of *Much Ado About Nothing* have both been performed and treated as if they were the original versions, and the English plays were mere translations of them. Who can really say for sure?

Throughout the films, and the various series, the influence of Shakespeare was constantly highlighted, from TNG to Discovery and DS9.

STAR TREK BARDS

Star Trek spawned its own collection of bards. Writers lined up to write books based on and in the *Star Trek* universe beloved and read by fans the world over. How do they do when placed inside *The Tao of Trek*?

As mentioned earlier, while many of these books are not considered canon, aspects of them have been adopted into canon in various ways. Bantam Books was the first publisher of *Star Trek* novelizations and tie-in fiction and did so from 1967-to 1994.

These fell into several categories, some more memorable than others. There were episode novelizations, some good and some bad, none ever adopted into the official canon.

But there was also a series of "Original *Star Trek* Adventures" based on TOS. These were published from 1970 to 1981 and included a favorite of mine, the James Blish novel, *Spock Must Die!* Sondra Marshak and Myrna Culbreath co-wrote several novels, and two volumes, *New Voyages*, and *New Voyages 2* that were both excellent.

The majority of these books aligned well with the general philosophy of Trek and Roddenberry. However, there were exceptions, and the series also spawned a lot of fan fiction that went far beyond the original journeys and intent of the series, even into romance and other storylines. Many are interesting as fan explorations go but are in no way canon or aligned with the original intent of the series.

Not all fiction is written under the auspices of the copyright holder, but some get a wink and a nod from the companies or creators. Fanfiction encompasses the efforts of fans of certain works to play in the world they love. Some prefer to create new characters and plots in a universe already well understood, while others use the existing characters to go on new adventures or explore relationships. This happens with every major franchise and innumerable more minor works, from *Harry Potter* and *Star Wars* to hundreds of anime series and TV shows. Trek is no exception.

Although characters, settings, and even plots have been used by other authors back as far as Shakespeare (several of his plays were based on stories by other authors) and Arthur Conan Doyle, modern fan fiction came into its own in the sixties when *Star Trek* fans published it in their fanzines (amateur magazines produced by fans). In fact, a common term for fanfic focusing on male homosexual pairings of characters, or 'slash', comes from these early *Star Trek* fanfics. Fans interested in 'shipping' (pairing characters in romantic relationships) Captain Kirk and Mr. Spock would term their stories 'Kirk/Spock', which they later shortened to just the slash between the names (or even their couple's name, which is often ironically stated to be Spirk). There's even a website called the KS archive and a convention called KiS con.

Star Trek allowed immense flexibility in creating fanfic, from 'shipping' characters who fans were interested in, to sending the *Enterprise* on new adventures and even creating new ships and crews to explore other parts of the galaxy. New authors could use fanfic as a way to hone their skills by eliminating the need to create a setting, characters, and plot from scratch. To practice writing skills alone, a fan could tell an existing story from the point of view of another character rather than the one used in the original.

Creating new stories with existing characters in the existing setting allows for improvement in the plotting and pacing of their writing. Imagining new characters in a well-known setting lets the writer concentrate on developing well-rounded inhabitants of that world. Writers can learn a lot from creating fanfic.

This isn't why most fans turn to fanfic, though. People want more stories from franchises they love, and fan fiction allows them to create stories tailored to their desires. If they prefer more action-oriented plots, they can write episodes where combat occurs. If they are interested in exploring certain characters and their relationships (as presented in the shows or as they imagine them), then many write romances or deeply psychological tales. The *Star Trek* universe offers a vast scope for fans to set their own stories in, and they've been taking advantage of that for over 50 years.

Authors like Vonda McIntyre stayed not only true to the series but to the philosophy of Trek as well and even had their works endorsed officially. McIntyre also novelized *The Wrath of Kahn*, *The Search for Spock*, and *The Voyage Home*, along with her original adaptive works.

There were even books based on TAS, novelizations that included material by Alan Dean Foster that tied the episodes together and were called the *Star Trek Log*. Rather than list all the various novelizations and series, instead we'll refer you to that section on our website, where we have assembled a list of all the books and the series they are in, and where you can potentially purchase them now, although your local library may have many of them. When I was young and living in a small town in Eastern Idaho, I was fortunate enough that one of the librarians at my hometown library was either a Trekkie or sympathetic to them because many of the books could be found on their shelves.

For the sake of our discussion, I would say this: most of the editors at the various publishers from Bantam at the outset to Simon and Schuster, Del Rey, and others were careful about the works in ensuring that they added something to the original or explored a different aspect of the world (like the *Star Trek: Rihannsu* series that explored Romulan culture during the timeframe of TOS), or expounding on implied adventures hinted at in the books and films that were a part of the canon.

Books are still being written based on the *Star Trek* universe, although not as many as there once were. However, as Trek experiences a new awakening with many new series and films in development, we will likely see a resurgence of fanfic and official books again.

MINSTRELS AND FILK

Outside of fandom, Filk is relatively unknown. Named after a typo in a convention program where 'folk singing' came out 'filk singing' fandom adopted it as the official name for this genre of music. As I (James) learned in the science fiction club I attended for many years, anything done once becomes a tradition. Filk is simply songs, original or based on existing music, with topics or lyrics dealing with science fiction or fantasy.

The songs from *Lord of the Rings* and the *Hobbit* (both the books and films) can be considered filk. So could the rewritten lyrics of "Jingle Bells" as sung by the Joker: ...The Batmobile lost its wheels, and the Joker got away! Much of Jonathan Coulton's music easily fits under the filk umbrella, including "Skullcrusher Mountain"; "Re: Your Brains"; "Still Alive"; and "Creepy Doll."

With the popularity of *Star Trek*, it comes as no surprise many filk songs are dedicated to it, but it might be surprising that some even entered the pop-culture consciousness. I would bet many people have heard and could even repeat a few lyrics from, "*Star Trekin'*" from the novelty band The Firm (not to be confused with the Supergroup of the same name). "Always going forward, still can't find reverse!" "There's Klingons on the starboard bow (starboard bow, starboard bow) ..." While marketed as a novelty song, and even characterized as highly annoying, it made the number one spot on the UK's Singles Chart and earned frequent replays on the Dr. Demento Show.

But that was 1987 and after. Ten years before that, Leslie Fish released "Banned From Argo," possibly the most popular *Star Trek* filk song ever. The song details the escapades of the crew of the *Enterprise* (although none of the crew nor even the ship herself are named in the song) as they set down for a few days of shore leave in Argo port. Most of the major characters get their own verse describing their misbehavior, with additional lyrics added by other filkers as time went on. Many convention filk circles banned "Banned From Argo" due to too many requests to sing it. In fact, Leslie Fish herself will sing it only once a year, usually at a major convention such as WorldCon, NASFIC, or DragonCon, as fans would request it repeatedly throughout every convention she attended.

In addition to this blockbuster, Leslie Fish released other *Star Trek-related* songs, such as "The Thousandth Man." The song speaks to the close friendship of Kirk and Spock, but the lyrics are taken from the Rudyard Kipling poem of the same name. Fish is well known for adapting Kipling poems to music for filk songs, such as "Engineer's Hymn", dedicated to Scotty. She also writes songs that other artists record. The filker Julia Ecklar sang "Iron Mistress" written by Fish, where Captain Kirk mourns the many women he loved and lost because of his dedication and love for his ship.

With so many songs written about *Star Trek* and its characters, I'd like to point out that much filk dedicates itself to space exploration in general. Songs such as Leslie Fish's "Hope Eyrie" about the Apollo moon landing carry hope and dreams about our future much as *Star Trek* imagines a bright future for humanity. And not all treat these things as fantasies.

I'd point to Sassafrass's song "Somebody Will" as an example. Rather than emphasizing the science fiction heroes, they take the point of view of one of us who can't contribute directly to these future victories. Each verse speaks of the everyday people who support space exploration even though they will never directly benefit from it. Though they know Mars has 'crimson dust waiting for footprints that will not be mine', they are still 'willing to sacrifice, something we don't have for something we won't have, but somebody will someday.' This intense optimism for our future reflects the optimistic tone of *Star Trek's* Utopian future.

In fact, the general optimism of filk and the minstrels who sing it sit well in *The Tao of Trek*. There is little that doesn't embody the ideas and philosophy set forth by Roddenberry from the very start.

But books and songs are not the only things inspired by the adventures of the starship Enterprise and the other parts of the series. Other fan-created work has emerged, and some of it has even resulted in battles with Paramount and the owners of *Star Trek* intellectual property.

OTHER FAN-CREATED WORK

For a long time, Paramount and the other owners of *Star Trek* content have been fairly liberal with their allowance of fan works, as long as it falls into certain categories and does not cross certain lines. But there have been two notable instances where the copyright owner took action, and fans in some cases became outraged.

So, what are the rules, exactly? Well, that is murky water and one reason you don't see a clear shot of the enterprise on the cover of this book, or a foreword by William Shatner or George Takei. There are contracts in place to prevent current stars and some past stars from participating in unlicensed work, which this book definitely is.

The biggest thing that tends to get the copyright violation machine running is to create something that could be substituted for watching the show or engaging with licensed products. For example, there are literally hundreds of unlicensed books, blogs, podcasts, websites, and other works not endorsed by Paramount or the Trek parent companies. These go on pretty much unimpeded.

Why? Because most point back to the original works, like this book does. There are no lengthy summaries of episodes, and if you are not a Trekkie, it is our hope that you become one, whether that starts with Old Trek or New Trek for you. Works need to be derivative and transformative, not copies of work done elsewhere, especially that which would be considered canon.

There are two well-known cases we can talk about here, both of which encountered unique obstacles.

The Joy of Trek: How to Enhance Your Relationship With a 'Star Trek' Fan

The first happened in 1998, and while there are clear reasons why the lawsuit went forward, there are also some subtext questions as well. Here's the story, summarized from the *New York Times* coverage. (24)

The book, The Joy of Trek: How to Enhance Your Relationship with a 'Star Trek' Fan was published by Carol Publishing Group of New York in 1997. Early in 1998, Paramount filed suit. They said that the author, Samuel Ramer, essentially summarized the show, gave detailed character profiles, and specifically summarized some episodes, meaning the book could serve as a substitute for watching the show.

Ramer countered, stating he created the book for his wife, whom he had recently married, who was not a Trekkie, to give her some context. And as a prosecutor for the state of New York, he felt he was legally in the right.

But to be fair to Paramount/Viacom, he did mention 220 episodes in the book, and as a result, the Paramount suit initially asked for $22 million, and sales of the book were halted (although there are copies still floating around). Essentially, a judge ruled that the middle 158 pages of the book were simply summaries of episodes and other books and didn't add anything new to the *Star Trek* universe.

Despite the fact that his motives were certainly pure, and his heart was in the right place, Ramer did, or so it appears, violate the intellectual property of Viacom and seek to compete with some of their own works.

This is perhaps the most well-known book violation. But if you are a Trekkie at heart, you know what we are going to discuss next.

Axanar and Who Owns Klingon?

Okay. So, for this, we need to remind you of a bit of background. Remember when Paramount and Viacom, both part of the same group, split the rights to television and films? Well, the two started to fight, and for a bit, this brought all Trek production to a halt.

And Viacom, unlike Paramount before it, decided to enforce copyright, sending cease and desist notices to unlicensed websites, blogs, and more. Because of (you guessed it) fan pushback, perhaps the modern equivalent of a letter-writing campaign, they backed off. Until...

Alec Peters proposed a prequel to TOS, Axanar, focused on the Four Years War between the United Federation of Planets and the Klingon Empire. It focused on Garth of Izar, a minor character who appeared only once in TOS.

But the film, and the *Prelude to Axanar*, a short 20-minute film with over 5 million views on YouTube (26), planned to follow canon quite deliberately, and the work clearly followed the Trek brand. For better or worse, this sparked pushback from Paramount/Viacom, and they filed suit. By this time, the Kickstarter for the professional-grade film has raised over a million dollars.

Fans, even Justin Lin, the director of *Star Trek; Beyond*, hoped the suit would be dropped, but the copyright holder pushed ahead. A judge ruled that the work was "substantively similar" to Trek, and due to how true to the world the creatives wanted to be, he wasn't wrong. Uniforms were similar. Garth was ruled to fall under copyright and to not be obscure.

The other issue the suits addressed was the use of the Klingon language. This did not resonate well with fans, however. Countless others have been a part of developing the Klingon tongue, refining it, and even translating Shakespearean plays and other works into it (as we mentioned above).

This made a part of the suit even more personal for fans who created fiction surrounding the Klingon species, their words, and their culture. The question they asked was simply: "Who owns Klingon?"

The judge left some of the other rulings to a jury but did state that "although the Defendants further argue that the Axanar Works, through their promotional value, actually increase the sale and visibility of the *Star Trek* Copyrighted Works. But 'the boon to the [latter] does not make [Defendants'] copying fair.'" (27) In 2016, production halted, although there remained hope that it would go on at some point. There were even fan events like Axacon created.

But in 2020, Gary Graham left the project due to "irreconcilable differences" clearly related to two things: pay, and the fact that Gary wanted to land a role in the new *Star Trek* series, *Strange New Worlds*, and his association with *Axanar* would hurt his chances of doing so.

So, while the fan film is far from "dead" and the show and the showrunner still have fans, it's unlikely the desired feature film will be made anytime soon. (28)

But there is a silver lining here because Paramount caused its own issues as well.

LEONARD NIMOY, HEINEKEN, AND PARAMOUNT

It's one thing to write a book like this one that is unlicensed, but there is something else entirely to running an unlicensed ad campaign. Such was the case when Heineken ran an ad featuring the image of Spock, with an interesting sexual innuendo. When a fan asked Nimoy about the billboards and posters, and he finally discovered them, that caused him to discover something else too.

Paramount had been using his image on lunchboxes, posters, and other places without compensation. So, he sued. And they finally paid up for the Heineken ad and other uses with very little fight.

Why? Because Nimoy refused to even look at the script for *Star Trek: The Motion Picture* until they did. A check arrived, he signed, and the rest is history.

What does all this have to do with *The Tao of Trek*? Well, clearly, there are times when the good of the many means the good of the fans, and while Roddenberry fed fans material for their works, the new holders of *Star Trek* rights clearly don't always feel the same generosity. Much of what fans do has always been technically illegal, but Paramount set precedent by turning a blind eye.

This was despite their own violations and how they took advantage of the talent on the show. So, while we strive for harmony, history has shown that part of Trek is taking a stand when needed. Writing letters. Pushing back when the very group that makes a franchise profitable is maligned or even mistreated.

This passion for a single franchise ignited fan-created works in other universes and worlds as well. And in that, Trek again changed the world.

Next, we'll explore another way that Trek changed the world forever: the rise of conventions, or cons, on a level never seen before and later imitated by the fans of other films.

CHAPTER 6
PROS AND CONS: TREKKIES YOUNG AND OLD

"The first duty of every Starfleet officer is to the truth, whether it's scientific truth or historical truth or personal truth! It is the guiding principle on which Starfleet is based! If you can't find it within yourself to stand up and tell the truth about what happened, you don't deserve to wear that uniform!"

— *Ronald D. Moore and Naren Shankar*

Depending on how deep into the fan community you are, you may or may not have heard of conventions. Conventions, or Cons, come in a variety of flavors, literary, media, Science Fiction, Fantasy, Furry, and specialty ones for specific topics, such as Doctor Who, Discworld, and, of course, *Star Trek*. These aren't a new phenomenon; the first World Science Fiction Convention (WorldCon) was held July 2-4, 1939, in conjunction with the New York World's Fair, so for well over 80 years, there's been conventions.

But the history of *Star Trek* conventions starts with *Star Trek* itself. Actually, a little before it, if you can imagine! During the "Tricon World Science Fiction Convention" (September 1-5, 1966, in

Cleveland, Ohio), Gene Roddenberry promoted his new Star Trek series, which would debut the following week. He even brought the first two pilot episodes. So, attendees of the 1966 WorldCon were the first fans to see "The Cage" (the original version) and "Where No Man Has Gone Before".

While there is some debate about the very first All-*Star Trek* convention (there are claims for the Newark Public Library holding one in March 1969), the first major Con was *Star Trek* Lives! in 1972 in New York City. Organized by a small group of fans, mostly women, they rented a hotel ballroom for January 21-23 and estimated they could attract a few hundred fans. By the end of the convention over 3,000 attendees had arrived to watch episodes screened from 16mm prints, see the now legendary blooper reel, view the art show, and participate in the costume contest. Guests at this early convention included Gene Roddenberry, Majel Barrett (Nurse Chapel and the voice of the Enterprise computer, and who married Gene later on), D.C. Fontana (screenwriter), and science fiction author Isaac Asimov.

The Committee was headed up by Joan Winston and others, although the chair was one Al Schuster, who later became a source of controversy. In 1972, it looked like this:

- Al Schuster, Coordinator
- Elyse Pines, Program
- Joan Winston, Dealers Room, NASA Display, Signs
- Eileen Becker, Registration
- Allan Asherman, Art Show
- Deborah Langsam, Costume Call
- Joyce Yasner, Displays
- Devra Langsam, Slide Shows, Program Asst.
- Regina Gottesman, Hospitality
- Steve Rosenstein, Auctioneer, MC
- Stu Hellinger, Program Assistant
- Chris Steinbrunner/Chester Grabowski, Visuals

Threheeeventefeatured several activities that would become standard convention features over the years, including episode screenings, a masquerade ("costume call," a forerunner of today's cosplay), and an art show. NASA even got in on the act, providing displays like an astronaut suit and actual moon rocks.

With such a successful beginning, the Convention Committee (ConCom) decided to put on more, and with more guests! Many of the regular cast members attended these Cons, drawing in even more fans. The 1973 Con had 6,000 attendees, and the 1974 Con had 15,000, with 6,000 more turned away at the door. In 1975 the Con went through some changes, including Al Schuster leaving the group under some controversy. This split the ConCom, and they limited attendees to 8,000.

These early Cons and the *Star Trek* 'Supercons' that followed them were run for profit, using the draw of familiar actors to bring in large numbers of fans, allowing them to sell dealer space to many specialty businesses who catered to *Star Trek* fans.

Seeing how many people came to these events, Hotels and other venues made sure they made a profit from renting their spaces. Celebrities wanted more money to attend them. The Cons were forced to bring in more people and dealers, raise prices, and sometimes to cut back on guests to lower their expenses. With the higher costs, fans began to move on to other conventions, such as Media Cons, which didn't limit themselves to a single franchise but branched out into many popular television and film properties. For-Profit conventions still exist, such as Creation Cons which have *Star Trek* specific Cons in addition to Cons for other franchises such as *Supernatural*, *Lucifer*, and

Stranger Things. Many other organizations running conventions to make money went under.

Media Cons (or multi-genre Cons) continue to be successful, with healthy amounts of cross-pollination between different fan bases to keep their Cons going. The most famous of these might be the San Diego Comic-Con and the many imitators who sprang up around the country and the world. Due to branding concerns, some of these have been renamed, but others such as Emerald City Comic Con (Seattle) and New York Comic Con retain the name. Many of these are run as nonprofits. One of the largest Media Cons in Europe, FedCon in Germany, originated as a *Star Trek* only Con in 1992 but later branched out into other related fandoms. Destination *Star Trek* Conventions, billed as Europe's Official *Star Trek* Conventions, are held in various locations such as Germany and the UK.

Perhaps the most numerous *Star Trek* related Cons are the fan-run events. When any motivated group of fans (or fen, the 'official' fandom plural of fan) can fund-raise and put on their own Convention, of course, they will! Libraries will host Cons as well, which fall more on the literary side of the spectrum but cover a wide variety of genres and media franchises. At any Convention, you are almost assured of seeing some sort of *Star Trek* presence due to its extreme penetration into pop culture.

So, what can you expect from a Con? The experience I hold highest, regardless of which type of Con, is the one of finding your band of friends. Only when attending a Convention, can you feel surrounded by so many people who will 'get' you. Everyone else attending has a similar niche interest that most people in their lives don't understand, but you will, even if you don't share that particular fascination. Star Wars and *Star Trek* fans are famously at odds, but they both understand the idea of being fans.

When I (James) attended WorldCon in Reno, NV, it was held in the Atlantis Casino's convention center. To get to the restaurants or hotel rooms from the Con, you needed to pass through the Casino. I'm not a gambler, so I really didn't connect with the people sitting in front of slot machines or walking down the halls unless they had the conspicuous Con badge hung around their neck. I immediately knew that person was part of my group as soon as I saw that. If I needed something, I could stop them and ask, knowing at least they would listen for a moment even if they didn't help. They weren't friends, but they were fans, and I knew they'd traveled here for the same reason I had. It was a strange experience returning to work afterwards. I worked in a large corporate campus where badges were required. It took a day or two to readjust and stop regarding those badges as signs of shared interest and remember they just meant a similar employment.

Another experience rare outside of Conventions is meeting the 'Pros' (Professionals, in the writing-oriented Cons I attend. These are the well-known authors, in *Star Trek* Cons, they can be writers, directors, producers, or actors). Unless you attend a *Star Trek* or Media Con, where else would you meet William Shatner? Or Zachary Quinto? Although 'meet' might be too strong a word. You can have one of these Pros sign a photo for you or get a picture taken with them for an additional fee. It's unlikely you'll be able to sit down and have dinner with them, though, or even visit over coffee or a drink, in the writing world, that's more common. You can buy an author a drink and chat in the bar for a short time if they are free. But actors are much more difficult to approach and much less likely to be able to spare the time. Cons assign special staff to run interference for their guests so they can make their appearances on time and aren't continually surrounded by hordes of fans.

Most Cons hold a variety of panels and talks where some aspect of the fandom is discussed. This could be anything from discussing how long it would take for the Enterprise to reach all the places visited in its five-year mission to what the most popular pairings of characters are in Fanfiction. This is another rare experience for fans. Most disagree on these topics, so spirited debates can emerge among the presenters, the audience, or between the two.

As I mentioned regarding finding the group you best fit into, fans of the series can get together and talk to one another. Many clubs have been formed by people meeting at Cons and exchanging contact information. What better way to continue celebrating your favorite show than to form a club to get people together all through the year. In fact, *Star Trek* even has its own dedicated club structure, STARFLEET International. Each local chapter is represented as a 'ship' crew.

And with this chapter, we end the first part of our work, the one that gives those who are not Trekkies the background of Trek, those who are a quick refresher, and a little bit of an idea of who the fans of Star Trek are and where they came from.

We've also talked about various works: books, songs, and fan-created work that's made Trek as much a part of the mainstream as it has become. This has allowed the philosophy behind Star Trek, from Roddenberry's original ideas to the evolutions that have occurred since, to become such an integral part of society.

PART TWO
THE TAO OF TREK

The pages that follow deal more directly with the Tao or the philosophy of Trek. As such, they contain a lot of opinions. These are things that you may agree with or you may not. They are not meant to be scripture, but interpretation as best we can divine of intent and perhaps application of these principles.

If anything, they are intended to spark discussion and even, in some cases, debate. We, as humans, tend to form strong feelings based on our own background and experiences, and as you will see, there are many discussions that take place in the Star Trek community around these various topics.

Whether you are a Trekkie or new to Trek, this is where we stop giving you the background of the show and start talking about the very things that make it special and enable the world of Trek to endure the test of time.

CHAPTER 7
THE PRIME DIRECTIVE: A MORAL COMPASS?

"The Prime Directive is not just a set of rules; it is a philosophy ... and a very correct one. History has proven again and again that whenever mankind interferes with a less developed civilization, no matter how well-intentioned that interference may be, the results are invariably disastrous."

-Picard, Symbiosis, TNG, Season 1, Episode 22

The Prime Directive exists to remind us that we are not gods. We don't get to reorganize every world, every civilization, every existence out here in our own image.

— Kirsten Beyer

~

By using the very title, *Wagon Train to the Stars*, Roddenberry defined for others what he really wanted *Star Trek* to represent, but it was something rarely seen in the human, earthly experience, peaceful exploration, and first contacts. In fact, the Prime Directive came out of his clear distaste for the Vietnam War and everything it represented. If we take an honest look at human history and where this very philosophy came from (and exists today), it tells us so much about who we are versus who we say we would like to be.

While this concept serves primarily to drive conflict in stories, its origin springs from the time the show began. The United States' involvement in the Vietnam War demonstrated how cultures could be steered from organic growth by the direction of more powerful nations such as the US and USSR. In addition to cultural contamination to create support for one superpower or the other, weapons and equipment were provided, disrupting the technological balance between each side. Producer Gene L. Coon is credited with introducing the Prime Directive concept during the Original Series.

As author Una McCormack has said, "The Prime Directive is a nice ideal, but have you noticed it never works in practice?" But why not? And why was it that so often, despite how important he stated it to be, Captain Kirk violated this most sacred rule?

Well, it goes back to the very origins of the idea itself.

Westphalian sovereignty is the name given the principle of national sovereignty embedded in international law, and a part of the charter of the United Nations, which states, "nothing ... shall authorize the United Nations to intervene in matters which are essentially within the domestic jurisdiction of any state." (11) Historians have traced the origins of this doctrine to the Peace of Westphalia (1648), which ended the Thirty Years' War. (12). But the philosophy reached its peak of popularity in the 18th and 19th centuries during the era of colonization and exploration.

But clearly, it faced challenges even then. We don't need to look any further than the colonization of Australia and other areas, namely the Imperialistic Era of England. Similarly, the conquest of the United States, including the American West, made it clear that although they considered themselves to be nations, the Native American tribes were not regarded as sovereign by the early colonists. These violations are recent history, and even today, Russia and China (think of the invasion of Ukraine occurring as this book goes to print) seem determined to take over countries around them, imposing not only their will on them but their culture as well.

Of course, there are other challenges, and these are often addressed in *Star Trek* itself. I mean, not interfering in civilization or culture is one thing, but allowing them to continue into extinction when it can be prevented? It sounds like a horrible thing to do. And in today's world, humanitarian reasons are often cited for interference in less developed nations and peoples.

But what of the historical record that shows us no matter how noble the motives, interference in the sovereignty of a people inevitably ends in conflict? How do we deal with those facts as they are? Here are some thoughts from, of course, *The Tao of Trek*.

WESLEY CRUSHER AND EDO

Look, as much as some hard-core Trek fans would not have wept had young Crusher been killed by the Edo for crushing some freshly planted flowers (TNG, "Justice", Season 1, Episode 8), Picard chooses to save him.

Since you already know what I think of season one of TNG, and now what I thought of young Wesley at that point, and that truthfully the Edo laws were ridiculous in both the plot and any connection to reality, Picard's violation seems forgivable. What is tough to swallow is the potential impact that had on the Edo society.

For example, if you enter almost any state in the United States, you submit to something called "implied consent." If you break the law, you are still criminally or civilly responsible from a legal standpoint. Ignorance is no excuse. Why? Because in this case, even the state laws are considered sovereign.

It was the same when the Enterprise crew encountered the people of Edo. Regardless of how ridiculous the law might seem to humanity, by beaming to their planet, the crew submits to their laws and culture. Defiance by an outsider may have inspired defiance by citizens after that, and who knows what the consequences were. (Thankfully, we never have to see that).

This is just one example of a violation from Picard.

WHO WATCHES THE WATCHERS?

In a similar series of events in Episode 4 of TNG Season 3, when the *Enterprise* reaches Mintaka III, a native of the proto-Vulcan society is critically wounded, and Doctor Crusher beams him to the ship to save him. The being catches a glimpse of Picard and understandably thinks he is a god.

This creates an interesting dilemma: do they leave the planet with this being thinking he has seen god? Surely that will change the direction of the culture. After a failed attempt to wipe his memory, Picard beams down and explains space travel to the citizens of this planet.

Which of these would have been a more significant violation of the Prime Directive? It's hard to say, but what we do know is that Picard chooses the purposeful violation over the accidental one that has already occurred. Was he right? Who knows?

OTHER CLEAR VIOLATIONS

Examples positive, negative, and neutral occur during the series, from the first season in 1966 through episodes of Discovery. In "Patterns of Force", a Federation observer intentionally introduced Fascist government policies based on Nazi Germany in an attempt to capture the efficiency demonstrated by this form of governance. This interference created a close parallel to Earth's own history, including racial prejudice and extermination of enemies of the state.

A more accidental impact happened in "A Piece of the Action", where a hundred years before the Enterprise arrives, a prior ship (sent before the establishment of the Prime Directive) left a book, *Chicago Mobs of the Twenties*, on the developing planet. The crew finds a planet ruled by gangsters and emulating 1920s culture. While technically violating the directive in an attempt to redirect the culture back to a less violent and derivative one, another accident leaves a communicator on the planet which will, of course, allow a significant advance in technology as it is examined.

Most positive examples of Prime Directive violations illustrate the tension between following the rules and doing the right thing. While in general, the Prime Directive protects cultures from contamination, in some cases, the cultures in question appear twisted and wrong, even self-destructive, and the audience sympathizes with the character's choice to interfere.

There are, in addition other violations of the prime directive. We see examples from Kirk (TOS, "Taste of Armageddon", "The Apple", and others), Janeway (VOY, "The Killing Game, Part Two" and many of her Delta Quadrant deals), and Sisko (DS9 "Let He Who is Without Sin" and "Captive Pursuit") to varying degrees. Of course, the worst offender is said to be James T. Kirk, who, according to some fans, "Broke the Prime Directive so badly, they almost couldn't put it back together." (13)

But what was the Prime Directive intended to do anyway? Richard J. Peltz argues in his article "Wagon Train to Afghanistan: Limitations on *Star Trek*'s Prime Directive" in the *University of Arkansas Law Review* that the prime directive:

1. Is not inviolable, rather its violation is inherent in its nature.
2. It is not a rule of law, rather an aspiration.
3. It is a product of a Utopian fiction, and as such, can never be fully realized on the Earth as we know it. (ibid. 13)

What does this mean for today, and how has the idea of the Prime Directive impacted us? More importantly, as we tackle *The Tao of Trek*, is there a way we can apply this to our own lives? The answer is a mixed "yes and no".

You see, the Prime Directive is an ideal, while something like the Hippocratic Oath is, well, an oath. And it is much more attainable. It is easier to get behind an edict to "do no harm" rather than "never interfere." And as Good Samaritan lawsuits often show when tested in court, the failure to act if you could do good things can be seen as just as bad as inadvertently doing harm in a negative situation.

For example, suppose you know how to perform CPR (whether your certification is up to date or not) and you come to the aid of a person in danger. In that case, you are typically protected by the law in most states and cannot be sued for any harm you inadvertently do in the process. (29)

We could compare this to another fictional law created by Isaac Asimov in his Laws of Robotics. The first law states that "A robot may not injure a human being or through inaction, allow a human being to come to harm." This law is designed to keep robots from getting out of control, and much of the conflict in Asimov's fiction comes from the conflicts these laws produce.

But for a moment, let's imagine that the Prime Directive instead states that a Federation vessel and crew may not allow a civilization to come to harm through the introduction of technology or knowledge beyond their current development, but also cannot, through inaction allow their civilization to come to harm.

This would, in some cases, allow the actions taken by a starship crew to save a civilization, even if that means revealing the truth about the Enterprise, the Federation, and space travel. The example above of "Who Watches the Watchers?" is a great example. Once the Prime Directive was violated, the choice came down to what would do the least amount of harm and enable the civilization to continue in the most peaceful manner possible.

Even if this were to change, and therefore justify some violations of the current Prime Directive, it would never excuse the sacrifice of a crew member to preserve it. The debate between the value of one over the good of the many would still come into play.

An example of this comes from the Kelvin timeline film, *Into Darkness*, where Spock must place a cold fusion device in a volcano to save a civilization from destruction, but in the process, the *Enterprise* is revealed to the natives. In part, this was to save Spock from the volcano.

In short, this and other examples reveal the two sides and the idealistic nature of the Prime Directive as something to aspire to, but that can never be followed as an absolute rule.

For now, we will leave this topic and talk instead, albeit more briefly than we would like, about the ways in which the show itself fulfilled (and the franchise continues to fulfill) the mission of the Enterprise to "boldly go where no one has gone before."

CHAPTER 8
TO BOLDLY GO

"It's not safe out here. It's wondrous, with treasures to satiate desires both subtle and gross. But it's not for the timid."

- Q

∿

Troy: One of the things I loved about Trek as a kid was the sense of adventuring into the unknown. I'll digress only briefly to tell a story or two from my childhood that epitomizes this.

I grew up in the southeastern corner of Idaho before the state got really "discovered", and there were a lot of unknowns to venture into. From summer canal surfing on plywood (ask me sometime, and I'll describe it, as I am no longer capable of demonstrating it) to wintertime sledding down hills so steep we had no business trying to navigate them on saucer sleds, we lived in a veritable world of the unknown.

And my imagination made it even better. Snowy fields became a new and unexplored icy planet. Desert was the surface of a blazing planet, where I, a brave exploring captain, had landed on behalf of the United Federation of Planets.

Not that television and Trek were my only source of space stories. I read all the classics, from Ben Bova to Asimov and Arthur C. Clarke, Heinlein to James Blish and his adaptations of Trek episodes.

We didn't have cable. My friend with a VCR was a Star Wars fan (thanks though Brad for letting me watch those films at your house), and he had cable. I relied a lot on books, the television at the babysitter's house, and more books. My local library was my second home, and I would check out stacks at a time.

And in the stories I wrote, hand pecking them out on the old Royal typewriter gifted from my grandfather, I clearly dreamed of space travel and, well, boldly going where no one had gone before.

There's more to that story. My family and my religious background discouraged my love of sci-fi. I didn't fully develop my inner geek or fully realize my fandom until I left home, and there's an infamous incident with my mom and her throwing away one of Heinlein's books from my collection.

But what resonated with me from the start was the very willingness to boldly go, and I believe Roddenberry clearly shared and showed that same passion. In the next chapter, we will talk about Infinite Diversity in Infinite Combinations (IDIC) and the impact that had, but first, we can talk briefly here about the impetus that made that possible.

A BOLD PREMISE

First and foremost, we can talk about the very premise of the series. As outlined above, the idea of the Prime Directive was born out of Roddenberry's hate for the war effort in Vietnam. It reflected his belief in its injustice and the needless loss of life.

But there was more. As we talk through things like IDIC and the need of the many outweighing the needs of the few, we are talking about what many saw as radical views on race and social construct.

One of these was the casting of Nichelle Nichols as communications officer Lieutenant Uhura. The truth is she planned to leave the show and pursue a career on Broadway. Who convinced her to stay? Martin Luther King, Jr. "Nichelle, whether you like it or not, you have become a symbol. If you leave, they can replace you with a blonde-haired white girl, and it will be like you were never there. What you've accomplished, for all of us, will only be real if you stay."

"That got me thinking," she said in an interview, "that this was bigger than me, bigger than all of us." Think about it. If she had left, the famous first interracial kiss on television would never have happened.

BOLD CULTURAL IMPACT

Everything from the letter-writing campaign that saved the series (at least the first attempt) to the first *Star Trek* computer game (1971) to an unprecedented fan convention (1972), everything about TOS was filled with bold moments executed by everyone from writers to directors to fans. These moments challenged the way we watch television, the way we do fandom, and the things we saw on the big and small screen.

Think of these amazing things that can be attributed to *Star Trek*:

- George Lucas, the creator of another popular sci-fi franchise that begins with Star, said: "*Star Trek* softened the entertainment arena so *Star Wars* could come along and stand on its shoulders."

- The first space shuttle was renamed *Enterprise* instead of *Constitution* after–surprise–a letter-writing campaign organized by Trekkies.
- Nichelle Nichols was recruited by NASA in 1979 to help entice more women and minorities to the program, resulting in more diversity.
- The TOS interracial cast, which we have already highlighted, was a television first. But the show also featured a Utopia where people of different races, origins, and even mixed-race individuals (the half-Vulcan Spock, for example) all worked together toward a common goal.
- The show offered a positive view of the future during the Cold War.

And those are just the impacts on culture. Roddenberry and the show's creators managed to predict:

- Cell Phones.
- PDA's and later Tablets
- New space propulsion methods.
- Communication breakthroughs like Facetime and other video calling.
- Streaming music and playing music on computers (and now phones). This was inspired by Data's easy access to his music on TNG.
- Non-invasive medical imaging techniques.

While certainly not the only sci-fi franchise to impact both culture and technology, *Star Trek* has done this in a big way and continues to do so. But there are other ways the show has boldly gone.

BOLDLY TAKING ON SOCIAL ISSUES

From the beginning, *Star Trek* took on cultural and diversity issues and more. From the first interracial kiss mentioned above to the diversity of the crew, from not-so-subtle references to things like the Vietnam War and later global conflicts, the writers and showrunners for the series have never been afraid to go beyond current television and film norms.

That continued beyond TOS to the "new Trek" (a term we will explore later). *TNG, DS9,* and *Discovery* all explored everything from same-sex relationships to non-CIS gendered individuals and other current cultural issues. *Discovery* also examines the issues with sentient AI when Zora, the ship computer, becomes self-aware and alters its own programming. *Lower Decks* is a clear exploration of the blue-collar workers of the future: those members of the crew in the lower decks that make everything work behind the scenes.

As always, we recommend you watch these shows and decide for yourself (currently streaming on Paramount+). And we want to hear from you. Because each of us, as Trekkies and fans, have been inspired, often to boldness, by the Trek franchise.

BOLDLY GOING BEYOND OUR SOLAR SYSTEM TO THE GALAXY

One thing Star Trek did for our imaginations was take us beyond our solar system in a visual way. Yes, there were books that spoke of planets outside our solar system and beyond the galaxy. And those in academia wrote of such things, but in an entirely theoretical and, well, academic way. TOS was one of the first television series that allowed us to see outer space in ways we never had before, from strange but inhabitable planets to the strange yet oddly familiar creatures who had evolved there.

The planets, the stars, the galaxies! From red earth to poisonous clouds, from new and unique resources, we were introduced to worlds much different than our own. As we are first exposed to them, we judge them by our idea of normal; twin suns, a sky that was not blue, more than one moon, worlds without oceans. All of them seemed alien to us.

There were also people and creatures who at first appeared monstrous ("The Devil in the Dark", for example) but turned out to be much more like us than we initially thought. Their cultural issues mirrored ours. The very principles we lived by were challenged, and we were occasionally reminded of how silly we really looked when viewed through a different lens. Through fiction, we were able to see our world, our society, and ourselves as we truly were.

These are the things Roddenberry and Trek continued to do so boldly. We are introduced to cultures both friendly and evil, good and bad, and like the planets they lived on, we judged them at first by our standards of right and wrong, our morality.

But we found something else. No matter where we went in the universe, humans were still uniquely, humanly flawed. But other races had their own strengths and flaws, and we were shown how we might not only understand them but be made better through that understanding.

In these explorations, we found something beyond the Laws of Humanity as we understood them. We found a much broader, universal morality.

BOLDLY GOING BEYOND RELIGION TO UNIVERSAL MORALITY

While we will tackle this topic in more detail in our chapter titled "Freedom from Religion", for the moment, we will just state that Star Trek boldly showed us that other creatures on other worlds also evolved and developed with a sense of right and wrong, good and evil.

Some ascribed to religion. Others did not. Some were warriors. Others sought peace. But throughout the Star Trek universe, we find that goodness is both praised and protected but can also be misunderstood. As we saw these new people, these new worlds, it was Roddenberry's vision that we would study, understand, and embrace those differences.

Which is why, in the next chapter, we tackle yet another bold declaration that would become a part of nearly all Star Trek from TOS to Discovery: the Vulcan principle of Infinite Diversity in Infinite Combinations.

CHAPTER 9
INFINITE DIVERSITY IN INFINITE COMBINATIONS

"["The Devil in the Dark"] impressed me because it presented the idea, unusual in science fiction then and now, that something weird, and even dangerous, need not be malevolent. That is a lesson that many of today's politicians have yet to learn."

— Arthur C. Clarke

"Intolerance in the 23rd century? Improbable! If humankind survives that long, we will have learned to take a delight in the essential differences between people and between cultures. We will learn that differences in ideas and attitudes are a delight, part of life's exciting variety, not something to fear. It's a manifestation of the greatness that God, or whatever it is, gave us. This infinite variation and delight, this is part of the optimism that we built into Star Trek."

— Gene Roddenberry

Our specific geographical location, Commander, is irrelevant. We continue to carry our cultures and backgrounds within us, no matter where we are."

— Peter David, Martyr

"Oh, I'm a great believer in IDIC, Commander: Infinite diversity in infinite combination[s]. The beauty of it is that nobody's wrong. Logic, Battle. They're all facets of the same thing. As if the true reality of the universe, whatever final answers there are to be discovered—if they can be discovered—is like a hyperdimensional string. Look at it one way it's an electron. Another way and it's a proton. Yet another one you can see a veteran. But it's all the same thing, just different ways of looking is all."

— Judith Reeves-Stevens, The Fall of Terok Nor

"Star Trek was an attempt to say that humanity will reach maturity and wisdom on the day that it begins not just to tolerate, but take a special delight in differences in ideas and differences in life forms. [...] If we cannot learn to actually enjoy those small differences, to take a positive delight in those small differences between our own kind, here on this planet, then we do not deserve to go out into space and meet the diversity that is almost certainly out there."

— Gene Roddenberry

∼

When it comes to precepts, this one comes with a little bit of controversy, not because of the principle itself, but how it was introduced to the original series. First, let's look at what the symbol and the "cornerstone of Vulcan philosophy" means.

Infinite Diversity in Infinite Combinations (IDIC) is actually a symbol, introduced through a piece of jewelry on Spock's uniform, introduced in season 3, episode 7 of the original series. The symbol includes a triangle within a circle: "The triangle and the circle are two different shapes, materials, and textures. They represent any two diverse things which come together to create truth or beauty, represented by the jewel in the center," as stated by Mr. Spock himself (Season 3, Episode 5 "Is There in Truth No Beauty?").

This part of Vulcan philosophy, considered by some to be the cornerstone of it, refers to the infinite diversity in infinite combinations that is and must be a part of the beginning of the universe. This coincides with the Vulcan idea that all creatures are to be equally respected, along with all races. The origin can be traced back to modern Vulcan philosophy founder Surak (introduced in the original series season 3 episode 22 "The Savage Curtain" in which Kirk, Spock, Abraham Lincoln, and Surak attempted to help a rock creature understand the concept of "good vs. evil."

The Vulcan word for IDIC is *Kol-Ut-Shan* (Voyager episode "Gravity"), but fans also often use other terms like *t'triahve*. In Traditional Golic Vulcan, the term used is *Va'Vuhnaya s'Va'Terishlar*. Another term for the concept is *Kol-uchang*, according to *The Vulcan Language Guide*. (20)

But the philosophy, and the use of the symbol, although it originated in the original series, also was frequently referenced elsewhere. In the TAS episode "The Infinite Vulcan", Kirk uses the concept to convince Spock 2 not to defy the concept by forcing his philosophy on others. And IDIC played a big role in the overall Vulcan belief that the needs of the many outweigh the needs of the few. This is, of course, illustrated dramatically in Wrath of Khan, the Voyager episode "Endgame," and in the Enterprise episode "The Council."

What stirred the controversy, then? Well, it turns out Roddenberry wanted to introduce the concept and the jewelry in the "Spock's Brain" episode that ran just before "Is there in Truth No Beauty?" This was a rare occurrence for the creator in Season

3, but his motivation was more about selling the pins than the original philosophy of *Star Trek*.

His modifications for "Spock's Brain" were rejected by the director, probably related more to a tight filming schedule than anything else, so he added the jewelry, and a scene explaining it, to "Is There in Truth No Beauty?" Of course, this was a last-minute addition, and both William Shatner and Leonard Nimoy saw the commercial ploy and refused to do the scene as Roddenberry had written it. Nimoy called the producer Fred Freiberger, who came to the set first, and when he wouldn't act, phoned Roddenberry himself. (1)

"To his credit, Roddenberry was completely honest about the situation and didn't try to mask his free publicity scam behind any half-baked creative half-truths," Shatner recalls in *Star Trek Memories* (2). "So I went through a great deal of soul-searching and teeth-grinding over the situation, and finally I just had to say, 'Gene, I'm sorry, but I can't do this.' Roddenberry accepted my refusal but kept working on Leonard."

Of course, Nimoy himself was unmoved. "Certainly, I was all in favor of the philosophy behind the IDIC-- but not the fact that Gene wanted me to wear the medallion because he wanted to sell them through his mail-order business, Lincoln Enterprises. Where the scene had been problematic creatively for me, it was now problematic ethically. While I wouldn't argue with the IDIC concept, I was troubled that I had opened the door and let in a new kind of animal while trying to get rid of another."

Eventually, Rodenberry postponed the scene to later in that week's filming and re-wrote it. Although still not a fan, Nimoy and Shatner did it anyway, although Nimoy still described it as "a rather unpleasant experience."

Roddenberry stood by the scene, though, and its inclusion. He said this:

"The inclusion of the IDIC in that script was valid. I truly believe in the statement -- in the message behind it -- Infinite Diversity, Infinite Combinations. Why wouldn't I want that in the show? In that episode, in particular, because of the woman character having studied on Vulcan. And then taking that philosophy and making it available to the fans was something I wanted to do. Imagine the power of that -- kids wearing that and explaining to their parents and their peers what it meant. To be able to get those kinds of ideas across to people who might not have ever seen the show was worth doing. Look, tie-in merchandising is part of the business of television. We had it from the start of *Star Trek*, with toys and comic books, the ship model, and the record albums. Leonard didn't see how making those records was a form of exploitation, but he felt that marketing the IDIC was. He missed the point. If we were going to sell anything, it should be something with a positive message and philosophy behind it." (14)

How does this relate to *The Tao of Trek*? Well, much like other philosophical ideas that are good in their content and even their nature, their introduction can often be self-serving and even tainted. Perhaps we can even take a lesson away from this. After all, *Star Trek* has given much to the world: the philosophy of IDIC just being one of the most valuable of precepts among those gifts. But there is always an exchange. Roddenberry, like many others, was motivated extrinsically along with his love for the series and the ideas behind it. He needed to, intended to, and certainly did profit from it.

Little could he have imagined, on that set Tuesday, July 16, 1968, how much IDIC would come to mean to fans in future days, series, and how it truly would become a cornerstone of Vulcan philosophy, one that valued logic over emotion, and that so often put Spock in difficult positions.

The IDIC symbolism would also continue to be featured in future Trek series, including VOY, ENT, and Discovery. But at times, it has been misinterpreted by fans and others alike. The true meaning, according to Roddenberry, rests in the truth that "beauty, growth, and progress all result from the union of the unlike."

Others have taken it to mean that there is a place for all opinions, but that simply isn't the case. There is no room for bigotry or bias in the philosophy of IDIC. All differences are equal, and none are lesser than any others. Infinite diversity does not refer to every ideology and opinion, especially those that want to eliminate diversity. Instead, it means "unending diversity."

That means any new race we discover, or who discovers us, no matter how different their culture and appearance. IDIC doesn't mean you have to suffer hostility or intolerance, for those go against the basic underpinning of the philosophy.

Then there are questions of how far Trek has gone and how far it should go. There is a lot of diversity in the series, including the LGBTQIA+ characters throughout. However, there are still many groups who are underrepresented in Hollywood and television, and the future worlds of *Star Trek* are the perfect places to take on those challenges.

As is tackling current events and challenging issues in society today. Roddenberry tackled the remains of World War II, Vietnam, and the peace and love movement of his time. *Star Trek IV* mirrored the end of the Cold War and what might come next.

And as with any philosophy based on a fictional ideal, it is more challenging to live IDIC than it is to declare it. But many Trekkies have undertaken the challenge to try.

And in that way, we can change the world yet again. But next, we will tackle something else IDIC must allude to: faith and its ongoing role in human history. For while *Star Trek* tries to display a world free of religion due to Roddenberry's adamant atheism, faith has been a part of human existence from the start, and it was often portrayed in both favorable and less favorable light in the original series.

But what does that really mean when we put it into practice in *The Tao of Trek*?

CHAPTER 10
FREEDOM FROM RELIGION

"I handed them a script and they turned it down. It was too controversial. It talked about concepts like, 'Who is God?' The Enterprise meets God in space; God is a life form, and I wanted to suggest that there may have been, at one time in the human beginning, an alien entity that early man believed was God, and kept those legends. But I also wanted to suggest that it might have been as much the Devil as it was God. After all, what kind of god would throw humans out of Paradise for eating the fruit of the Tree of Knowledge?

One of the Vulcans on board, in a very logical way, says, 'If this is your God, he's not very impressive. He's got so many psychological problems; he's so insecure. He demands worship every seven days. He goes out and creates faulty humans and then blames them for his own mistakes. He's a pretty poor excuse for a supreme being."

— *Gene Roddenberry*

"On a show about diversity and with different points of view, I feel like you have to accept that some people believe in God, some people want to worship a potato, and some people don't want to believe in anything. I think there is room for that on Star Trek."

— Gretchen Berg

"There are seven billion people on this planet. As many as six billion pray and meditate, and never look at a book on reason, logic, and math. Imagine if, instead, these six billion people were literate in reason, logic, and math. If that were the case, we would already be building starships and making Star Trek for real rather than as a TV show."

— Mark Romel, The False Awakeners: Illusory Enlightenment

"If Captain Jean-Luc Picard asked you to serve him aboard the starship Enterprise, you'd likely be happy to. You would recognize him as a great leader and a good man, and so you wouldn't have any problem following his orders. This is basically the relationship God wants with us - not slaves, not pets, not possessions, we would be co-workers and friends."

— Lewis N. Roe, From A To Theta: Taking The Tricky Subject Of Religion And Explaining Why It Makes Sense In A Way We Can All Understand

∼

Ah, religion. As taboo as politics at your in-laws' Thanksgiving dinner, it's a hard topic for anyone to discuss. But discuss it we will, or rather the absence of it–sort of–from the Trek franchises, and how Roddenberry thought it should be handled.

There are even some of the quotes above that could be seen as offensive to some. Gretchen Berg's reference to those who might "believe in a potato" could potentially offend someone who does have a strong belief system they embrace. And the Mark Romel quote? Not everyone has access to the tools needed to become literate in reason, logic, and math. The world is not an equal playing field. Even among those with such access, religion and faith are still present and strong.

Troy: In short, this chapter is potentially the most debatable in this book. To give you some background, I grew up in a very religious household. Note that I say religious and not Christian or spiritual because I have learned that those are two very different things. But while I was growing up, my immediate family members were not fans of my penchant for sci-fi. Why, you ask?

Well, my sci-fi heroes were none other than Isaac Asimov (an atheist and definitely a guy who believed in evolution), Robert Heinlein, and the esteemed L. Ron Hubbard. I even read *Dianetics* back in the day and realized it was just an odd form of Christianity with engrams instead of confession. Sort of. But I digress.

Because what we are going to talk about is *Star Trek*, sci-fi in general, and the assumption that as humanity evolves, they will grow beyond the need for religion. But when more primitive cultures are encountered, religion is often still present. It's portrayed as a crutch for people to explain things they just don't understand.

However, that doesn't work in the real world or in fiction. The Vulcans are very spiritual beings, and Spock's Christ-like resurrection on Genesis is just one example of the breaking of what I will call the "religious wall." And as we look around the world, as the quote that started this chapter states, of those on this planet, a huge majority worship something, meditate, and ascribe to some religion or another.

James: On an even more personal level, I am not particularly religious, but I did attend services with the Unitarian Universalists a couple of times. Besides being informed that the Wiccans attended the early morning service and listening to a talk on the details of the Clinton health plan by an actual doctor, there was a surprising talk about one person's 'perfect minister'.

The speaker told us the perfect minister would be a combination of Aunt Bea from *The Andy Griffith Show* (the character, not the actress who played her) and Mr. Spock. The loving and always caring Aunt Bea would provide the human warmth and empathy any good minister needs. On the other hand, Mr. Spock represented the logical side: the part of a minister with the thoughtful ability to analyze and look at the problems in his own life and those of his parishioners and devise solutions.

In his mind, both mentalities were necessary to provide a complete solution to helping people in crisis.

And even in the United States and the United Kingdom, where more people ascribe to atheism than anywhere, we see an incredible curiosity about the supernatural: ghosts, demons, angels, and all manner of other things we cannot explain through science.

In addition, although not particularly Jewish, it is interesting to see the number of Jewish undertones in the show. This likely comes from the fact that several writers on the original "*Star Trek*" series were Jewish, including the author of the popular episode "The Trouble With Tribbles" (David Gerrold). Both Leonard Nimoy and William Shatner were sons of Ukrainian Jewish immigrants — and the show tackled topics like racism and the Holocaust in both veiled and explicit ways. When Nimoy was asked in 2001 about the fundamental Jewish themes in "*Star Trek*," he answered with a list: "Social justice, meritocracy and the idea of *tikkun olam* — the healing of the universe."

There are many more cultural references that combine the principles of the *Tao of Trek* with those of popular religions. Dozens of news articles ("Was '*Star Trek*: The *Next Generation*' ... a statement on Jewish identity?"), as well as dissertations ("Golem as Metaphor"), podcasts (*"Star Trek* and the Jews"), and even other exhibitions ("Jews in Space") have explored the common religious threads that run through the show. Trekkie rabbis have even offered courses to their congregations, airing episodes like "The Enemy Within" (TOS) to illustrate the internal battle between good and evil.

It's also a universal truth that no matter how advanced we get with both technology and science, there will continue to be things we don't understand: the miraculous, the paranormal, the supernatural, and those pesky secrets hiding in Area 51.

So, you would think this would mean little to no mention of human religion in the series, right? But that surprisingly does not hold true: when we look at seasons and episodes, we see countless references to belief in God or gods by various crew members.

The Original Series

- The wedding chapel on the Enterprise contains an altar surrounded by various religious symbols. ("Balance of Terror")
- In the TOS episode "Metamorphosis", when the Companion takes over Nancy Hedford's body, Spock objects, "Companion, you do not have the power to create life." Companion-Nancy replies: "That is for the Maker of all things.", referring to the existence of God.
- "Scotty doesn't believe in gods", Kirk declares. "Man has no need for gods. We find the one quite sufficient". It almost sounds like the Captain ascribes to monotheism. (TOS: "Who Mourns for Adonais").
- The rebels on Magna Roma, a "Parallel Earth", seem to worship the sun. More precisely, Spock states: "Sun worship is usually a primitive superstition religion."

Uhura corrects him: "Don't you understand? It's not the sun up in the sky. It's the Son of God." ("Bread and Circuses").

- In "The Ultimate Computer", M-5 declares: "Murder is contrary to the laws of man and God.".
- There is also a mention of a Christmas party in "Dagger of the Mind."

Post TOS

- Data mentions a Hindu Festival of Lights in a log entry in "Data's Day." So theoretically, the religions, their festivals, or at least the memory of them, persists.
- In "Sub Rosa", the Caldos Colony (clearly Scottish in nature) includes a church or chapel beside the graveyard, and the attendees say "Amen" at Felisa Howard's funeral, clearly a part of a Christian ceremony.
- In the film *Generations*, Captain Picard celebrates Christmas with his family in a very traditional fashion, even by our current standards. This is odd considering it takes place in the dream world of a man who otherwise doesn't ascribe to a religion.
- Kilana asks Sisko: "Do you have any gods, captain?" He says, "There are *things* I believe in." (DS9: "The Ship").
- Joseph Sisko recites from the Bible to his son's surprise. Joseph also appears as a priest in Ben's hallucination (DS9: "Far Beyond the Stars").
- In the Voyager episode "Spirit Folk", the Doctor acts as a Roman Catholic priest in a holodeck scenario. This is the first time in *Star Trek* that a human religion is an integral part of the story.
- In the episode "Cold Front" of *Enterprise*, Dr. Phlox says he visited a Tibetan monastery and attended a mass at St. Peter's Square. The same doctor appears as a priest at

Porthos's funeral in one of Archers's hallucinations in the episode "A Night in Sickbay."

And these are not comprehensive lists. Far from it. When you add alien religions in the mix, some of which look all too familiar, we see that Trek, despite Roddenberry's ambitions, is not entirely areligious. And while in TOS and other early shows, religion is often presented as an obstacle or a problem overcome by science, it is certainly not always that way.

In fact, DIS deliberately sought to bring faith back into the franchise in the episode "New Eden", according to showrunner Alex Kurtzman. (Season 2, Episode 2) The concept of belief was in mind as a theme from the very beginning of planning for season two. "In the original series, religion doesn't exist," he says. "Yet, faith is something that has always been a major topic in different ways. The idea of this mystery that has no answer immediately suggests a presence or force greater than anything anyone has ever known. It was really intriguing to us."

According to "New Eden" episode director and TNG star Jonathan Frakes, this theme is timeless. "The idea we're all naive to believe there's not a higher power out there applies to the 24th century as much as it does to the 21st."

The entire episode deals with the conflict on the ship and the New Eden planet between logic and science and faith and belief. (To learn how it all works out, you'll have to go watch for yourself if you haven't already).

However, what this episode and other references in *Discovery* (such as the Red Angel in the final episode of Season 1) show us is the evolution in the Trek franchise over the years. We see here, as in many other areas, how society has impacted *Star Trek* and how *Star Trek* has impacted society. Perspectives on faith have been altered.

"We've evolved as a culture a lot since Gene Roddenberry was with us," Frakes told *The Hollywood Reporter.* "We have to stay current on so many levels, in the filmmaking and storytelling." (15)

The truth is that one of the reasons *Discovery* chose to deal with the issue of religion head-on is that boldness to stay relevant. But what's the danger?

The biggest danger of religion is that it takes something good, including moral principles and standards to live by, and makes them into something else, something they shouldn't be. For example, in this book, we are outlining *The Tao of Trek.*

That Tao certainly includes elements of the Trek franchise that we, and many other Trekkies, want to incorporate into our lives. They include the principles we have talked about so far and others. We want to work to build a world of:

- **Infinite diversity and harmony with all people**, regardless of their race, sexual orientation, gender, religious affiliation, and many more. We want to strive to embrace Infinite Diversity in Infinite Combinations.
- **Being bold in what we do**, in embracing the future, and in innovating to make it better.
- Creating a world of kindness and freedom from scarcity. (more on that in the next chapter)
- **Offering meaningful work for everyone**, whenever possible. This includes automation, worker safety, and equality among occupations, even those who work on the "Lower Decks."
- **Living in a society of peace**, where war is not our first response, but rather, as Asimov famously said, creating a world where "Violence is the last resort of the incompetent."
- **Realizing the good of the many truly does outweigh**

the good of the few (in most cases, and we will get to talking about that)

- **Wishing everyone the ability and freedom to live long and prosper.**

And this is not an exhaustive list. However, what is key to remember is that although these are precepts, things we have learned and taken away from this great body of fiction and can apply to our lives, it is not ever intended to be a religion.

- You can't get ordained as a Priest or Reverend of *The Tao of Trek*.
- There will be no churches or temples.
- While we encourage community gatherings (aka cons), there are no Tao of Trek meetings, sermons, or passing of offering plates.
- This book and any derivative works are not scripture of any kind.

That's because one of the very tenets of this work is the freedom from religion and to genuine belief, whatever that looks like for you. From science to spiritualism, what you believe is your business.

Because religion tends to take infinite, wondrous, and good things and tries to put them in a box, house them in a building, and pretend to know for certain the Creator's intent. And that is a true tragedy.

With that, we'll move on to one of the greatest achievements in the society of the Trek franchise: an era post-scarcity and where kindness is the rule rather than the exception.

CHAPTER 11
POST SCARCITY AND KINDNESS

"Roddenberry's dreams, Star Trek's dreams, help us to think through what it would be like to have a society of abundance, of logic and reason, and of inclusion."

— Manu Saadia, Trekonomics: The Economics of Star Trek

"If being human is not simply a matter of being born flesh and blood, if it's simply a way of thinking, acting, and feeling, then I am hopeful that one day I will discover my own humanity. Until then, I will continue learning, changing, growing, and trying to become more than what I am."

— Lieutenant Commander Data

~

E arly on, it is clear that in Star Trek, money is pretty much a thing of the past, at least in Starfleet, and poverty is no longer around. That frees people to explore their talents and creativity without worry of – well, going broke.

The thing this does is push greed out of the way and let us see a glimpse of more human motivations, like justice, innovation, and doing things solely for the good of many rather than just to get that new house or a flashy car. Such things mean little to nothing in this world, and while there are moments when those who are hungry for power display some of that greed, it is much less widespread and common.

Rather than the way things work in the real world of today, instead there is an abundance of goods and resources available to the people living there. While the shows focus on Starfleet, where food, clothing, and housing are all provided for its personnel, it is assumed that most citizens of the Federation have enough to eat, somewhere to live, and other necessities.

Poverty applies only to those groups outside of the Federation, usually found on another world. Some episodes are built around rushing medical supplies or specialty crops to other planets, but these are an exception and often due to plagues, famines, or other natural disasters. Even the fact Starfleet is able to rush these items to help shows its support for a minimum standard of living everywhere. Emergency assistance is given even those who are not a part of it when needed.

This illustrates, without preaching or hitting us over the head with it, that the Federation and the world of Star Trek are post-scarcity civilizations. Technologies such as food replicators indicate power is cheap and can be used to supplement people's diets easily. While our current world struggles with distributing adequate food to every person on the planet, a post-scarcity society produces ample goods to eliminate starvation and hunger without visible strain on the infrastructure.

The ability to produce more than adequate goods and services for everyone impacts society in profound ways. While in comparison, there may be rich and poor, the poor do not live in poverty but are simply unable to afford the same luxuries as the rich. With no necessity to take jobs which take time and energy away from their lives without adequate return, citizens of the Federation focus on self-improvement and performing work that enriches their lives.

In Starfleet, many characters are well-versed in complex hobbies, well educated, and generally happy. No one feels stuck in a dead-end job or the need to adjust their work/life balance. Their lives balance naturally, with ample opportunities to advance, learn, and grow.

Many in our modern lives speak about 'doing what you love, loving what you do' and finding your passion, but these sentiments contradict the paycheck-to-paycheck lives most people lead in many first-world countries. Some countries have even less opportunity to fulfill these types of dreams as their lives are a daily struggle to simply survive. While it's true we don't have the profligate production assumed in *Star Trek*; we can provide enough to assure everyone in the world is fed and housed. But this doesn't happen. With waste, the concentration of wealth, and other artificial barriers, we continue to see starvation, homelessness, and poverty. *Star Trek* provides a beacon to steer our world toward one where we've solved these problems.

Many of these problems show up in our daily news. Cities, where houses sit empty, are reported side by side with a growing homeless community. Employers are unable to find enough workers while immigrants eager to work are turned away at the border. Food is wasted in stores and restaurants while people go hungry.

That is not to say that there is no work being done on potential fixes. Laws pass which lower or eliminate sales tax on food and other necessities. Social support systems such as Welfare, Food Stamps, and housing subsidies exist and sometimes grow as more people are in need. Proposed systems such as Universal

Basic Income and Universal Health Care would work to provide the essentials in equal measure to everyone living under that government. And better skills training and education, and a new approach to work hope to eliminate planned obsolescence.

While we cannot yet produce the abundance we need to eliminate all these social ills, we can make a start. I hope we don't have to wait hundreds of years for our post-scarcity future.

Think of it this way. There is no room for waste on a ship and no opportunity for it. Water is distilled and created as needed. Food is created in appropriate portion sizes that are not wasted. Things that can be are recycled. Clothing is provided for everyone, even if that is in the form of a uniform or the dreaded red shirt.

Entertainment is also widely available and is equally elaborate for everyone. No one is spending dollars or credits to "rent" holodeck spaces. Instead, they simply schedule a time there.

A great example of this is *DS9*. While there are times when the station is short on rations, no one starves. We also see this in *Discovery*, when non-Federation worlds are in need, and the Federation finds a way to feed them in most cases. While we do see poverty, it is often the result of an oppressor who seeks to concentrate both wealth and power.

In fact, there are several books and various web articles about Trekenomics and the Trek Economy. (16) However, I don't think they exactly cover the topic adequately. Here's why:

First, there appear to be private, small businesses in the Trek world. For example, Quark's bar in *DS9*. There is also Sisko's restaurant in New Orleans and Chateau Picard, to name a couple. But what do they have in common?

Well, first, both of the latter produce things that theoretically cannot be replicated, at least not exactly. A replicator produces food but not necessarily a home-cooked gourmet meal. I mean, if I could get some Franklin's BBQ from a replicator...but I digress. Red wine and the nuances of taste from a particular vineyard would likely be difficult to replicate, and it's also unlikely replicators would be programmed with such delicacies.

Everything from Romulan ale and various other beverages to exotic food dishes would come from human effort. Not everything can be replaced by technology.

Also, the theory of *Trekenomics* is based on the fact that as technology advances, it gets cheaper and easier to manufacture and produce the goods that satisfy everyday needs. They include food, shelter, and clothing. However, as we see in our own world, until we decentralize wealth and create a different kind of consumer culture, even though we can manufacture some things cheaply and easily, not everyone has access to them equally.

Think of the very idea that as of this writing, houses can be 3-D printed from concrete, made of hay bales, old tires, and other readily available materials, including shipping containers. However, we still have an affordability crisis in housing due to supply and demand, not the actual value of those goods.

Post-scarcity involves both technological advancements and an attitude shift about the ownership of goods and, at its core, the very nature of our lifestyles. And one of those often raised to idol-like status is the idea of a career and work.

But in the world of Trek, meaningful work is the norm. Or is it? We'll look at that precept next.

CHAPTER 12
MEANINGFUL WORK

"A simple, magnificent equation: ingenuity plus hope equals change."

— Una McCormack, The Last Best Hope

"But notice that the writers aren't necessarily saying it's a good thing or a bad thing...only that it wasn't Boimler's thing. He is more "at home" on the Cerritos, even though it's not the Titan or any of those other action-packed ships that are constantly fighting. He even says earlier in the episode that he'd rather explore the galaxy than shoot his way through it; that's why he joined Starfleet in the first place.

And frankly, that's my truth, too."

– Jonathan Lane, Fan Film Factor Blog

∿

T o illustrate the principle of meaningful work, we are going to look at one of the newer additions to the *Star Trek* franchise, *Lower Decks*. That is because this show, more than most of the others, focuses on those we would have considered red shirts in TOS, those afraid to be chosen for an away team with leadership. These are those we call in our modern society Essential Workers.

Star Trek: Lower Decks is set in 2380 after *Nemesis* and *Voyager* returned to earth, is a comedy that might at first look like a spoof but isn't. In fact, creator Mike McMahan states that Lower Decks is canon, meaning things that happen on this series could, in theory, affect other shows.

But rather than focusing on ship leadership like captains and chief medical officers, this series focuses on "lower deck" life. These are crew members who perform menial, everyday tasks that are necessary but certainly not glamorous. The starship itself, the *USS Cerritos*, is a relatively unimportant ship in Starfleet. The series is named after the episode with the same title in TNG season 7, episode15 which focused on ordinary *Star Trek* personnel.

While animated, the series definitely leans more adult, like the *Rick and Morty* series McMahan also created. It's more comedic than any other *Star Trek* series, and the time it is set in (at least in season one) is a relatively peaceful one for Starfleet (five years before the Synth Revolt on Mars and seven years before the Romulan Supernova of 2387). The ship's mission is described as "second contact", meaning after other starships make first contact, they come in and "find all the good places to eat and set up communications."

It's almost like following around the support vessel for an aircraft carrier in the *Top Gun* franchise. Those ships are always there, but they're not important enough to get any screen time. The series has been greenlighted for a third season already in production. So far, the show has tackled things like:

- **Synth Labor:** there is some synth labor not previously seen in *Star Trek* canon outside of flashbacks in Picard, but because of when Lower Decks is set, it makes sense that some is present.

- **The Borg:** Hinting at the fact that the Borg might still be active somewhere, the second episode features a training simulation called The SmorgasBorg to train Starfleet officers on failure. Apart from what we have learned from Picard, we don't know what that means (yet).
- **Cybernetic Enhancements:** Rutherford has recently undergone cybernetic enhancement. This was formerly frowned upon by the Federation, except in life-saving circumstances. We don't know enough to know whether laws have changed or if there is a backstory to Rutherford; we don't know yet.

What do fans think of *Lower Decks*? Well, it has a reasonable rating on Rotten Tomatoes, but the series debut seems to almost immediately polarize fans. Some love the irreverent quirkiness of the show, and if you take it on its own, that works.

For background, the crew is largely unimpressive, as is the troubled lead character, Ensign Mariner, who gets away with a lot of insubordination and the kind of behavior that would get you sent to the brig on *Enterprise*. However, that is by design: these are the lowly grunt workers of Trek on what is at first deemed an unimportant ship tasked with a relatively benign mission.

But if you are looking for the earnest, hopeful, best-of-humanity and other races present on the other *Star Trek* series, *Lower Decks* at first seems to miss by a mile. Cleaning out the food replicator is much less hopeful and dramatic than saving the entire crew by sacrificing your own life (*Wrath of Kahn*, anyone?). However, just because they are not out saving the universe does not mean they are not enriching their lives. And that is really what Star Trek is all about.

THE PRECEPTS OF *THE TAO OF TREK* (NOT) IN ACTION

So, unlike many of the other series, in this case, there is not a whole lot of sacrifice happening along the way. In fact, there is a lot of selfish behavior, although there are some friendships formed which could morph into greater themes later.

A good example is episode one, Second Contact, where we are introduced to Ensigns Brad Boimler and Beckett Mariner, who happens to be the daughter of the Captain, Carol Freeman. Boimler is summoned to the bridge, a rare treat, and asked by the Captain to report breaches of protocol by her daughter, who she wants to have removed from the ship. The only heroism is accidental: Mariner is caught giving equipment to local farmers, a clear no-go. Boimler is attacked by a local farm animal and covered in slime after his uniform is destroyed.

Meanwhile, the crew is unwittingly infected with an alien virus by Commander Ransom, and they all start to fight the other members of the crew. Boimler is beamed up, and the Chief medical officer T'Ana uses the slime he is covered in to synthesize an anecdote for the rest of the crew.

Is there friendship here? Well, kind of. After he lies to the Captain for her, Mariner agrees to help Boimler achieve his dreams of becoming a captain. Was there a sacrifice for the good of others? Sort of. Kind of an accidental one, really.

Fortunately, in the opinion of some fans, the show gets way better in this respect.

THE ESSENTIAL WORKER

The thing is, cleaning out the food replicator is not nearly as "sexy" on screen as doing battle against a Klingon warship, but as Boimler himself says in Season 2, Episode 2, "Kayshon, His

Eyes Open" of Lower Decks, "I'd rather explore the galaxy than shoot my way through it; that's why I joined Starfleet in the first place."

And what we learned in 2020-21 and beyond, those workers in the lower decks of our world are, first of all, essential to our everyday lifestyle. Secondly, many feel their work is extremely meaningful. If you've ever gotten a horrible cup of coffee at a national coffee chain with your name spelled wrong on the outside, you understand.

It may seem like a small thing at the time, but it can set the entire tone for someone's day. And what historically will become known as the "Great Resignation" (if you are reading this in the future because an English teacher forced you to, look this up. It's one of the reasons you get an annual COVID-19 booster along with your flu shot) many of these essential workers are not only leaving their jobs but their professions as well.

In the wider Trek universe, we see that nearly everyone has a job that is considered to be meaningful work and that they enjoy. Automation, AI, and other wonderful technology has eliminated many mundane jobs that can be completed with greater safety by a machine. This is true of Starfleet and the United Federation of Planets, as clearly on other worlds, such work still exists.

If you are wearing a red shirt, of course, your job is a bit more dangerous. But when we really think about it, our world is already populated with meaningful work, we have and are developing technology that flips burgers and makes pizza for us, and we're even working on automating delivery.

We're not eliminating jobs, we're creating more meaningful work with greater opportunities, much like the industrial revolution, and *Star Trek* is just a world beyond this one.

In that way, the *Lower Decks* may be, as some fans claim, the only real *Star Trek* series happening right now. And the show has turned out, now two seasons in and counting, to be less polarizing than Discovery or the Abrams films. There are fewer outright haters.

Maybe it's the humor. Maybe it's the inclusion of more characters we can relate to. In fact, in a great blog on Fan Film Factor, Jonathan Lane claims to have figured out *Lower Decks* and why we all love it so much. The four main characters are the four types of *Star Trek* fans, and we love them so much because we have lived with them our entire lives. (17)

BACK TO MEANINGFUL WORK

All that was a long way to get back around to the topic of meaningful work. Here's the beauty of the *Star Trek* world, and while yes, it is fiction, and yes, it is aspirational, in the show, all work is meaningful, and this is possible for a very specific reason:

On a ship, even a modern naval ship, there is no room for waste and no desire to take along unnecessary personnel. If you do, you must support them with food, living space, toiletries, and more. This is even more important on a starship, where support includes things like oxygen and other life support.

It is only in a world of plenty where laziness is even possible. Unemployment on a starship? Please. They'll find you something to do to earn your keep. Not showing up for work? Critical in even what might be seen as the most mundane position.

And it may be prudent to mention Reginald Barkley here; a non-traditional Starfleet officer introduced first in TNG. He was portrayed as shy, socially awkward, and even suffered from holo-addiction, an addiction to the stories and worlds created by the holodeck.

As his character (played by Dwight Shultz) evolves, we see that when accommodations are made, we can see the brilliance of someone who was at first derided and had his fitness for duty questioned. More than once, Barkley helped to save the *Enterprise* (both D and E in TNG and later in VOY) or solve a thorny problem.

Someone seen at first as nonessential and perhaps even ill-suited for Starfleet became a most valuable member of the crew.

And all of that was a part of Roddenberry's vision. Think of the very name he gave the show: "Wagon Train to the Stars." The cook in a wagon train is equally important as the blacksmith or the hunter. Rank only refers to responsibility, not value or lack thereof.

And as we will see in the next chapter, all this meaningful work comes together for the good of the many.

CHAPTER 13
THE GOOD OF THE MANY

"Giving up our values in the name of security is to lose the battle in advance."

— *Christopher Pike*

"Some people view Gene as a man with a wild futuristic utopian fantasy, but that's too simple. Star Trek did not promise that people would magically become inherently "better," but that they would progress, always reaching for their highest potential and noblest goals, even if it took centuries of taking two steps forward and one step back. Ideally, humankind would be guided in its quest by reason and justice. The ultimate futility of armed conflict, terrorism, dictatorial rule, prejudice, disregard for the environment, and exercising power for its own sake was demonstrated time and again."

— *Nichelle Nichols, Beyond Uhura: Star Trek and Other Memories*

"You have been, and always shall be, my friend."

— *Mr. Spock to Captain Kirk*

"The needs of the many outweigh the needs of the few. Or the one."

— Spock, played by Leonard Nimoy

"Friends are friends," Brightspot said, *"whether I've known them for a long time or a short time."*

— Janet Kagan, Uhura's Song (21)

"I never knew what a friend was until I met Geordi. He spoke to me as though I were human. He treated me no differently from anyone else. He accepted me for what I am. And that, I have learned, is friendship."

— Data, Star Trek: The Next Generation

∾

While certainly not unique to *Star Trek*, the concept of sacrifice for the benefit of others is clearly emphasized throughout the *Star Trek* universe. A staple of storytelling, many characters put themselves in danger in the service of protecting others. Many militaries or police forces base their existence on this concept. But I would contend several staples of the franchise push this aspect to the forefront, making it clear this concept of service to others is a core belief of Starfleet.

A recent example comes from the first of the Kelvin Timeline films, in fact, the very beginning of that film where George Kirk is left in command of the *USS Kelvin* in an impossible situation. The Kelvin is completely outclassed by the ship they face and will inevitably be destroyed. Kirk orders the ship's evacuation by shuttles but stays behind to protect those shuttles from enemy fire and eventually ram the other ship to prevent it from pursuing the evacuees. He intentionally sacrifices himself for the lives of others, including his wife and newborn son.

This isn't an unusual plot point in a story, except that it ties to later concepts of the 'No Win Scenario' and the test the Academy runs called the Kobayashi Maru. For any non-fans reading this, the short version is: Starfleet ship gets a distress call from the Kobayashi Maru, finds the ship is in the neutral zone (Klingon originally, sometimes Romulan later), if they go rescue it, they get attacked with overwhelming force and destroyed. Basically, you can't rescue the ship; if you try, you die. And it's not really acceptable to ignore the distress call either. Here's another example of the actual Academy curriculum, including how to deal with a situation where you can't succeed. Where trying will cause you to sacrifice yourself, unsuccessfully, for others.

Most of the actual plots deal with ways people beat the no-win scenario, but the fact that it is so integral to a Starfleet education to know you may be faced with this situation emphasizes how important the concept is. Not only should you be prepared to lay down your life for others, but accept that sometimes even that, will fail. You'll die with nothing gained except the reassurance that you tried.

But where does this come from really? Well, it's the philosophy of utilitarianism. But is it really viable?

THAT IS LOGICAL

The good of the many outweighs the needs of the few, or the one, as the saying goes. This is a philosophy and like Spock's Vulcan heritage, a purely logical one. To reach any conclusion about an action, you simply weigh the outcomes by "what benefits the greatest number of people?" Spock clearly determined at the end of Wrath of Kahn that it was worth his life to save the lives of everyone on the ship.

Soldiers make these kinds of decisions on the battlefield; firefighters and other first responders make similar calls when they enter a burning building to save the lives of those inside. Those who do this in the face of very real danger are often called "runner-inners."

Our human survival instinct tells us when danger rears its ugly head to turn tail and run. Those who do tend to live longer, but many people considered "heroes' do the opposite. They run toward the danger to see if there is something they can do to help others, often risking their own lives in the process.

However logical it may seem, there is also a part of philosophy that states everyone has a right to life – their own. This is also true and logical in some ways. Although if we look at the situation on the Enterprise, everyone on the ship, including Spock, would have died if he (or someone else) didn't take action.

THE PROS OF UTILITARIANISM

The tradition of modern utilitarianism began with Jeremy Bentham (1748–1832) and continued with such philosophers as John Stuart Mill, Henry Sidgwick, R. M. Hare, and Peter Singer. The principle is simply that there are two essential motivators for humanity: pleasure or pain, and that pleasure or happiness is the greater good. The more people who are happy, the more noble the action.

There is also room for nuance. Think of a good workout or going for a run. There will be pain (go ahead and try it if you haven't in a while), but in the end, there are two forms of pleasure. The first is a kind of euphoria in the short term, known as runner's high, and a certain satisfaction in the completion of a difficult task, which gives us pleasure.

Also, there is long-term gain in health, mobility, and long life. The phrase "no pain, no gain" is directly related to utilitarianism. So, the philosophy is not about the avoidance of pain altogether, but the avoidance of pain that has no corresponding reward of pleasure or good.

For this idea to work, good must be defined and then adapted not just for the individual but for society as well. This is where things get tricky. The action of a government, for instance, that results in the greatest overall good for society as a whole may hurt some individuals in the society.

In fact, it almost certainly will. And this is where the downsides come in.

THE DOWNSIDES OF A UTILITARIAN APPROACH

Philosophers strive for an ideal logic, one that works in all situations, even on the *USS Enterprise*. The biggest issue becomes "who defines the overall good?" The smaller the situation, the easier it is to see the "greater good", but the larger the group of people affected, the harder it is to determine (without hindsight or a very large overall view) what that greater good is.

For example, if I am walking with my daughter and my grandchild down the street and a car speeds toward us, if I throw them to the side and sacrifice myself so they can live, you can say that is for the greater good: two people live who are younger and have a longer future ahead of them than I do. But what if, instead of me, it was a literal genius like Einstein or Tesla?

It could be argued that without one or the other of them, discoveries would still have been made, but perhaps not as soon, or the outcomes would have been different, and this is certainly true. But without some true and verifiable vision of the future, it is impossible to know who the child will become. What if in sacrificing himself, Tesla had enabled Jack the Ripper to live?

Yet this is a small situation. Spock sacrificed himself to save the *Enterprise*, but what if the destruction of the ship would have warned others of a much greater danger, thus saving millions of lives? Outside of fiction, there is literally no way to know.

Such thinking was used to justify the use of nuclear weapons on Japan and is often applied to the arguments about social welfare and more. We can see that much like the Prime Directive, knowing when utilitarianism works and is the best approach to adhere to and when it does not is an ideal: aspirational, but hardly achievable.

THE RULE OF LAW?

This brings up yet another point of philosophy: the rule of law. For if, like the Prime Directive, this "rule" that the good of the many always outweighs the good of the few or the one, then where does that leave other laws? When is it okay to break one to adhere to another?

There are countless examples throughout human history, and there will likely be thousands more in the future. We cannot see with hindsight until events have passed. The Utilitarian approach would say that logically dropping a bomb that killed several thousand was worth preventing millions of deaths. But the rule of law would tell us that to use a nuclear device to target civilians is wrong and a war crime in and of itself.

At the time, the commander, the ruler, if you will, can only see what is in front of them. They cannot see the future, and by the time they are able to see the events as history, they can only determine the morality of their actions when it is too late to change them.

Thus which approach is correct is impossible to know for certain at the time the decision is made. The decision-maker must trust one approach or the other and deal with the consequences as they come.

WHAT WE CAN LEARN

As with many other topics in this book, we could write an entire volume on the Good of the Many vs. the Good of the Few, the Hedonic calculus behind the Utilitarian philosophy, and how we could use such tools to move forward and make better decisions in our lives.

But instead, we are only looking at how this plays out in the world of *Star Trek*, and there are countless examples from the various series and shows. And we can see how this has impacted our society in the very examples given above.

And once again, we see the aspirational nature of *Star Trek*. For no matter how much we like to think we are logical beings, we also come with emotions and often subscribe to ideology (like the rule of law mentioned above). And for some, that ideology moves them toward war, more of a TOS Klingon view than that of the Vulcan race.

One of the things Roddenberry worked to show in TOS was his opposition to the Vietnam War and war in general. How Utilitarianism deals with that is actually mixed, as we have explored. Largely though, the original five-year mission was indeed about peaceful exploration and contact.

But some will say that much of the "New Trek" is as much about war as it is exploration. But as has been asked many times, "War, What is it Good For?" And more importantly, for our discussion, where does war fit into *The Tao of Trek*?

CHAPTER 14
WAR, WHAT IS IT GOOD FOR?

"We're Human beings with the blood of a million savage years on our hands, but we can stop it. We can admit that we're killers, but we're not going to kill, today. That's all it takes. Knowing that we won't kill, today."

— Robert Hamner, A Taste of Armageddon

"The president has listened to some people, the so-called Vulcans in the White House, the ideologues. But you know, unlike the Vulcans of Star Trek who made the decisions based on logic and fact, these guys make it on ideology. These aren't Vulcans. There are Klingons in the White House. But unlike the real Klingons of Star Trek, these Klingons have never fought a battle of their own. Don't let faux Klingons send real Americans to war."

— David Wu

"Beware of more powerful weapons. They often inflict as much damage to your soul as they do to your enemies."

— Greg Cox, The Rise and Fall of Khan Noonien Singh

From the beginning, *Star Trek* showed mankind exploring the universe. From the early elevator pitch ("Wagon Train to the stars!"), stories revolved around venturing to new lands and seeing what was out there. There were often plots involving diplomacy or rushing medical supplies to colonies, not to mention investigations of the disappearance of other explorers, but the exploration of "strange new worlds" stayed critical enough that it repeated in the credits of every original series episode.

It's not so much the exploration that epitomized the show, though. It's that these voyages were carried out with peaceful contact as their primary goal. Of course, as an action-adventure television show, contact rarely went as planned, and the ship and crew fought many battles with a variety of foes. But contrast this with historical exploration, such as Spain and Portugal's exploration of the so-called "New World" (although it was not new to those peoples who lived here). Their goal was conquest and gold. Anything that stood in the way would be overwhelmed. The exploration of North America opened new lands for settlers to occupy, regardless of who or what already lived there. Even famous scientific voyages, such as Darwin's trip on the Beagle, carried weapons and aided in putting down revolts in ports they visited.

THE IMPORTANCE OF SHIELDS

While the *Enterprise* did carry weapons, I believe their most important combat-related technology was their shields. They often used them to defend themselves, wherein a more real-world setting vessels require additional 'defensive' weapons to protect their ship. Modern warships carry systems like the Phalanx cannons to shoot down incoming missiles since we have nothing like *Star Trek*'s force fields (at least not yet). That these cannons can be used to attack others as well means even the most peaceful ships in the fleet are dangerous and potentially deadly.

Along with their Phaser's 'stun' setting, discussed later, the shields show that Starfleet is prepared to defend itself without escalating confrontations. This preparation indicates their emphasis on peaceful encounters during their explorations. While warships might bristle with weapons, Starfleet ships limit these and emphasize defense.

MISUNDERSTOOD INTENTIONS

While we talked about this a little bit in the chapter on peaceful exploration, it bears repeating here that so many conflicts in TOS, in particular, are a result of misunderstood intentions or cultural differences. Think of how you would react if a few Starfleet officers, dressed oddly and apparently armed, materialized in your neighborhood.

In the state where we both live, it would not be unlikely to hear shots fired or even elicit an armed response from local police. Regardless of peaceful intent, the unfamiliar is often seen as hostile. Even in the case of wild animals, often "attacks" on humans are caused by a misunderstanding. The mother bear considers the man to be a threat regardless of why he wandered between her and her cub (don't do this, by the way).

But think about even in our limited experience in our world on earth, how often conflict has come from differences in appearance, culture, or customs. Most religious persecution falls into this area, as well as things like the Salem witch trials. Why would space be any different? The simple answer is it likely wouldn't. Other races may perceive us as hostile simply because we look different and are strangers.

REVISITING BUDDHISM AND *THE TAO OF TREK*

As we stated at the beginning of this book, maybe the aspirational ideal of Trek would simply be this: That just because someone is different does not mean they are evil. We already discussed how this is clearly illustrated in TOS Season 1, Episode 25, titled simply "The Devil in the Dark."

Just because the creature's actions were hostile did not mean the creature itself had some kind of hostile intent. In fact, its actions were taken in self-defense.

It is also important to remember that all of us are the heroes of our own stories. We can easily justify our motives if we try hard enough, and that allows us to do almost anything unless we apply some simple life principles.

These principles are clearly expressed in the Buddhist philosophy and most directly in the principle of non-attachment and achieving enlightenment. As we stated before, the very principles of Buddhism make war an unnecessary evil. (22)

And this bridges nicely to our next topic, that of military weaponry in Trek.

A TASTE OF ARMAGEDDON: MAKING WAR "CLEAN"

Part of what we hate about war is how genuinely ugly it is. Even this is addressed by Trek in the twenty-third episode of the first season, "A Taste of Armageddon". Essentially two planets are at war, Eminar VII and a neighboring world, Vendikar. The war is conducted as a computer simulation, and those "killed" in the action are then disintegrated in real life as part of a treaty between the two planets.

If you're not familiar with the episode, it is a must watch. Spoiler alert: in the end, Kirk destroys the war simulation computers. (Another clear violation of the Prime Directive). One of the ambassadors, Anan 7, tells Kirk how wrong his action was. He states that it is natural to make war, and without computer simulations, they will have no choice but to conduct a real war.

But Kirk's counter is priceless. Instead, he argues that in being isolated from the horrors of war, the societies have no reason to stop it. He convinces them to initiate a cease-fire and negotiate peace.

Another important note from this episode: the thing that saved the *Enterprise* from an attack? Their shields. It wasn't the use of weapons that solved the problems of these planets in the end, but the fact that the ship had the needed protection to survive an attack without the need to counter.

THE ADVANCEMENT, OR LACK THEREOF, OF MILITARY WEAPONRY

When we apply this principle to the larger military establishment, we see a stark difference between our society and that of Starfleet. Without getting overly political, we can examine the way our overall philosophy has evolved.

You see, the United States became involved in foreign wars at first only to protect ourselves, then to protect "democracy around the world" in the quite proud and incorrect assumption that democracy was "the answer" regardless of the culture or country we encountered. From there, we moved to "eradicating anyone who moves and acts against us, anywhere." Simple examples: Desert Storm one and two, our involvement in Afghanistan, and to a lesser but similar extent, our involvement in Vietnam.

Another example is our defense of Israel (whether you agree politically or not) regardless of how we perceive their actions. The reason has more to do with "common enemies" than the actual protection of like allies. In a way, it is not "logical" but can be illustrated by the unification of the Federation and others against a common enemy throughout *Discovery* (and if you haven't seen it, I won't spoil anything for you).

The most common enemies in the Trek universe are both Klingons and Romulans, although we see in TNG and beyond where there is also an uneasy peace with them, and Romulan and Klingon individuals have been granted a place in Starfleet just like any other species. The two species have a different philosophy from the outset though: the way to take their place in the universe is not through peace but through war and the desire to conquer.

Set against the backdrop of the Cold War, *Star Trek* offered a bold take on the alternatives.

REVISITING THE PRIME DIRECTIVE (BRIEFLY)

We discussed in a previous chapter that Starfleet enacted General Order 1, better known as the Prime Directive, as a means of preventing contamination of alien cultures by more advanced civilizations, such as the Federation. Although never quoted on TV or film, it's clear all Starfleet personnel are familiar with the directive.

In review, while Picard in The *Next Generation* describes it as a philosophy, the order stands as a rule whereby officers who violate it can be removed from command or held for court-martial. In broad terms, it states Starfleet officers will not introduce more advanced technology or foreign concepts into other civilizations, primarily cultures more primitive than Federation worlds.

While imperfect, the idea of restricting more advanced civilizations, whether technologically or culturally advanced, from interfering in the development of others addresses many historical abuses that often resulted in war.

Much of history documents wars and conquests which occurred due to technological superiority or more efficient social organization. The Roman Empire held an advantage over others by perfecting military tactics and creating transportation systems connecting their empire. Spain and Portugal used their monopoly on firearms and armor to conquer and loot cultures such as the Incas and Aztecs in the Americas. Colonists in North America fought the indigenous tribes, taking their land and eventually restricting them to reservations. Obviously, the defeated cultures did not grow and develop naturally after their collision with more powerful adversaries.

Current advocacy against Colonialism shows this problem still weighs on people's minds. The balance between setting rules and doing what's right becomes ever harder to find as the world becomes more complex. As Kirk put it when defending his actions in the Kelvin Timeline film *Star Trek: Into Darkness*, if he hadn't interfered by stopping the volcanic eruption, that culture would have had no future. Is it ethical to interfere if you are saving a culture? What if you are only saving some lives? Where does one draw the line where your urge to do what you feel is right overwhelms your commitment to a moral principle?

SET PHASERS TO STUN

A line repeated often in the Original Series, using only the non-lethal setting of their weapons, emphasizes the desire to make peaceful contact with other races and cultures. But looking even deeper into this attitude reminds us not only are the phasers set only to stun their opponents, but that weapons technology expressly created a non-lethal setting in the first place. While obviously, future technology can create more and more devastating weapons, both personal and strategic, at some point, research diverted to finding a way to minimize the damage done and create a means of defeating and capturing foes without serious injury.

Our own weapon development shows some investigations into these capabilities, such as tasers, stun guns, rubber bullets, and various chemical irritants (tear gas, CS gas, pepper spray). But they seem far inferior to the stun setting.

Most modern non-lethal weapons inflict some injury either as their primary function or incidental to it. Chemicals cause pain and discomfort upon use and for some time after. Rubber bullets simply reduce the lethality of bullets while still causing physical injury. Electroshock weapons may inflict pain as their primary purpose or as a side effect, as well as burns, punctures, and inducing heart attacks. This is a far cry from stunning victims and putting them to sleep.

And an interesting thing happens throughout the various *Star Trek* series. Computers adapt and even become sentient (Zora, *Discovery*), propulsion evolves (hello Spore Drive), medical technology gets better, but weapons stay pretty much the same. Phasers and phaser rifles have two settings: stun and kill and are most often set to stun. Photon torpedoes and lasers are pretty much the extent of ship-level weaponry. Both are essentially what we would call "line of sight" weapons and are generally used only to target engines or weapons systems, not to destroy vessels.

Despite advances in other technology, more effective ways to kill are not a priority, as far as we see. Shields, even cloaking devices, are intended for defense more than offense. Compared to our "defense spending" and love of weapons development, it's–different.

But the movement toward removing the threat of lethal force being used against our own citizens has some proponents today. In some countries, such as England, the typical police officer does not carry a deadly weapon, while in others, such as the United States, the vast majority of police, and even most private security guards, are armed, some with multiple weapons. Many US police departments make the taser a standard issue for their personnel, along with a pistol, so officers have options when attempting to deescalate confrontations. But as protests against deaths and severe injuries caused by the police gain more supporters, it is obvious this isn't sufficient.

The phaser can actually, in some contexts, be compared to the Swiss Army Knife. While firearms are simply a tool for delivering an object at high velocity in order to injure or kill a target, a phaser presents a much more versatile set of features offered by the two settings since they appear to have varying power levels inside of those settings. Phasers used on the shows cut through metal like a welding torch, warm rocks to create a heat source, vaporize obstacles like fallen rocks, all in addition to stunning or killing opponents. Faced with wilderness survival, I'd much rather have a phaser than any firearm, even if it was somehow locked out of the lethal setting.

The same technology used in the simple, pager-sized phaser scaled up to a handgun, a rifle, a cannon, and a ship-based primary weapon, all while retaining this immense flexibility. In the original pilot, a phaser cannon cut away at the elevator leading to the cells where the aliens imprisoned Captain Pike. In "A Piece of the Action", the ship's phasers stunned a several-block radius defeating an attack by a rival mob. A flexible weapon indeed!

With such versatility available, it demonstrates the Tao clearly that most armed confrontations are begun with the command "Set phasers to stun." While Starfleet's weaponry allows for the use of overwhelming force, the assumption in almost every case is to use the minimum force necessary. Confrontations with hostile forces require protecting yourself, but by using stun settings these don't result in bloodbaths, and later negotiations are colored with the philosophy that it isn't necessary to kill because we disagree.

THE CAPTAINS OF PEACE

Finally, before we leave this chapter, it would be remiss of us not to mention the people behind peaceful exploration and preventing war. Just because they have phasers and photon torpedoes as their disposal, weapons that could cause real damage and initiate battle, they have one thing in common: their mission.

Most of the time, the captains of the various starships choose peaceful contact and negotiation ahead of war, and only respond in self-defense, usually with an attempt to disable rather than destroy their enemies when possible.

We need more leaders like that: those who, despite the power at their disposal, find that the most powerful path is to use that power for good, and only respond with war and violence as the very last resort.

In fact, the argument for peace and against war leads us to the Vulcan blessing, comfortably included in Leonard Nimoy's final tweet before passing in 2015: LLAP. Live Long and Prosper.

CHAPTER 15
LIVE LONG AND PROSPER

"How could there be any part of space that "belonged" to any specific species, because space had always been and would always be, long after the races that had staked their claims had vanished."

— *Peter David, Q-In-Law*

A life is like a garden. Perfect moments can be had, but not preserved, except in memory. LLAP

– *Leonard Nimoy, in his final Tweet, 2015*

Gene Roddenberry let Leonard Nimoy shape the details of his character, and Nimoy famously came up with the Vulcan salute from a boyhood memory of sitting in a synagogue and seeing the hand gesture used by the Kohanim, or priests, as they blessed the congregation.

The priests actually perform the action with both hands, touching their thumbs and forming the Hebrew letter Shin. This is the first letter of the word Shaddai, one of the names given to God in the Torah. When developing the Vulcan greeting, Spock only used one hand.

The sign itself is hard for some people to do because of the manual dexterity required, and this was even spoofed in *Star Trek: First Contact*. Some actors have even had to have their fingers glued or taped together for filming when required to offer the greeting. The gesture is intended to stand for the Vulcan "blessing" of Live Long and Prosper.

The gesture and the accompanying blessing were first used in TOS episode #2 (Amok Time) in 1967. The Vulcan language version, *"dif-tor heh smusma"*, was first spoken in *Star Trek: The Motion Picture* in 1979. The less common response, or sometimes the thing said first, followed by "live long and prosper", is "peace and long life."

While the source of the hand sign is pretty clear, that of the phrase itself is much murkier. Some point to the connection with Shakespeare and Romeo and Juliet, in Romeo's declaration to his servant: "Live and be prosperous: and farewell good fellow." This would certainly align with the final moments of WoK and Spock's dying farewell to Kirk.

A more detailed example can be found in George Du Maurier's *Trilby*, published in 1894, and a work that popularized the principle of a Svengali, or one with an unnatural control over the actions of another. A description of an art student ends with, "May he Live Long and Prosper."

Many believe the greeting is actually just the shortened version of the longer Jewish greeting the Kohanim, the Jewish descendants of Aaron, gave with the symbol itself:

The Lord spoke to Moses. Speak to Aaron and his sons this is how you bless the people of Israel, say to them;

The Lord will bless you and protect you, the Lord will go kindly and graciously with you. The Lord will bestow his favour upon you and grant you peace. Thus, they shall link my name with the people of Israel, and I will bless them. — *the Bemidbar, Chapter 6, verses 22-27*

Despite its significance in their religious practice, many Jews have never seen the sign in person. Because when the Kohanim offer the blessing, the congregation is supposed to look away. The intent is that the congregants should be focused on the words being said, not who is saying them or what they are doing.

According to Rabbi Morrison of the Beth Emeth Synagogue in Toronto, Ontario, "You're not supposed to look when the Kohanim do the blessing and 'salute,' because you are supposed to be focusing on the words and thinking of God as opposed to focusing on the people saying the words."

There are varying beliefs as to why one should turn away, and some appear to be stories told to children to keep them from peeking. Nimoy was told you could die for seeing the feminine side of God appearing during the blessing. In fact, Nimoy himself told startrek.com in 2012 that:

"I grew up in an interesting inner-city neighborhood in Boston. The area was known as the West End and was written about in a book called the Urban Villagers. It was a desirable area since it was within walking distance of downtown Boston and the Boston Commons, as well as being situated along the banks of the Charles River.

The population was mostly immigrants. Maybe 70% Italian and 25% Jewish. My family attended services in an Orthodox Jewish Synagogue, or "Shul." We were especially attentive to the high holidays, Rosh Hashanah, the Jewish New Year, and Yom Kippur, the Day of Atonement.

Since I was somewhat musical, I was hired as a young boy to sing in choirs for the holidays, and I was therefore exposed to all the rituals firsthand. I still have a vivid memory of the first time I saw the use of the split-fingered hands being extended to the congregation in blessing.

There were a group of five or six men facing the congregation and chanting in passionate shouts of a Hebrew benediction. It would translate to "May the Lord bless you and keep you," ...etc.

My Dad said, "Don't look."

I learned later that it is believed that during this prayer, the "Shekhina," the feminine aspect of God, comes into the temple to bless the congregation. The light from this Deity could be very damaging. So we are told to protect ourselves by closing our eyes.

I peeked.

And when I saw the split-fingered gesture of these men... I was entranced. I learned to do it simply because it seemed so magical.

It was probably 25 years later that I introduced that gesture as a Vulcan greeting in *Star Trek,* and it has resonated with fans around the world ever since. It gives me great pleasure since it is, after all, a blessing." (19)

This principle has indeed become one that permeates all of *Star Trek* and fandom, in everything from a greeting to a parting blessing, and one referenced more than once by Yo-Yo Ma during performances (he is a major Trekkie himself).

This greeting is used both in serious situations and with deep meaning and in more casual Vulcan interactions. It could be seen as like the Catholic and later protestant call, and response of "Peace be with you" nearly always followed by "and also with you." Both are offered in both formal and informal settings.

Whatever the origin, the intent is a sign of well wishes from the emotion-free people of Vulcan. But it often evokes a lot of feeling in the humans who are its recipients.

It does illustrate that in the half-human and half-Vulcan Spock, logic does not have to eradicate feelings and friendship. In fact, that logic itself can lead to personal sacrifice and a show of loyalty and friendship, things that on their surface are not always logical when viewed individually.

Of course, this also ties to the overall peaceful mission of Starfleet, and we must assume, like in many instances of military endeavors, that in the original five-year mission, we see only the moments of drama, conflict, and adventure that make great stories. Surely there must be many instances never recorded other than in the Captain's log: empty, dull planets, moments of peaceful contact quickly established, mapped, and moved past.

In those moments, whole civilizations, worlds, and races were left behind: left to live long and prosper, as *The Tao of Trek* drove the Enterprise and her crew onward. And this is now more clearly illustrated in the series *Lower Decks* where, as discussed above, the ship serves as "second contact" and the rather mundane tasks that go with it.

For most of us Trekkies, the Vulcan hand sign followed by the greeting "Live Long and Prosper" is just that: a greeting and a blessing of sorts as well. It identifies us as part of a tribe, one much larger than ourselves. We wish each other the best, regardless of where we come from politically, religiously, or otherwise.

It's a way of embracing Infinite Diversity in Infinite Combinations, and it can help us as we develop our own aspirational and practical Prime Directives.

But some question if some of the newer iterations of Trek in the franchise have upheld these values in their truest sense. And we'll look at that next.

CHAPTER 16

NEW TREK: NOT YOUR GRANDFATHER'S STAR TREK

"The gentleman who plays it in the new Star Trek films is great, but he's acting. Leonard was Spock. He was always the character."

— Edward Gross, *The Fifty-Year Mission: The Complete, Uncensored, Unauthorized Oral History of Star Trek-The First 25 Years*

"I sympathize with the guys who went to see The Phantom Menace and convinced themselves that it wasn't as bad as it was. Phantom Menace is worse, I would argue, than Star Trek ever was, but we were kind of in denial. There were some beautiful shots of the Enterprise and we got to see some Klingons, so it wasn't a total disaster, but in large part it was pretty boring."

— Edward Gross, *The Fifty-Year Mission: The Complete, Uncensored, Unauthorized Oral History of Star Trek-The First 25 Years*

"Genius doesn't work on an assembly line basis. You can't simply say, "Today I will be brilliant."

— *Kirk "The Ultimate Computer" Stardate 4731.3*

"Curious, how often you humans manage to obtain that which you do not want."

– Mr. Spock, "Errand of Mercy"

∼

There seem to be two clear eras of *Star Trek*, and really more, as we discussed earlier. To review, there are the following divisions in the release of films and series.

- The original series era: 1965-1969
- The post original series rebirth: 1969-1991 (this is when I first became a Trekkie)
- Post Roddenberry television era: 1991-2005
- Rebooted film series: 2005-2016
- Expansion of the *Star Trek* Universe: 2017-Present

Most fans would agree that there is definitely a split of the "Old Trek" vs. the "New Trek." The question is, where does this division happen in the eras outlined above. And what's the difference?

Common dividing lines for New Trek could be: anything post-Roddenberry, anything from the rebooted film series forward, or the newest Trek and the expansion of the *Star Trek* Universe.

It's easy to argue that in each of these instances, the Tao, or essential belief system of *Star Trek*, has changed in one way or another. So, for the sake of the Tao, we're going to explore for a few moments not how *Star Trek* has changed society but how society has influenced *Star Trek* and the essential Tao behind it.

Finally, before we close out this section, we'll talk about what we, as Trekkies and fans, can do to alter the future course of Trek.

THE EVOLUTION OF NEW VS. OLD TREK

First, before we address the actual divide between New and Old Trek, and what might be causing it, and how to fix it, there is something else we need to address. That is that New vs. Old Trek is an argument as old as…well, Start Trek the *Next Generation* back in 1987. Arguments included:

- "The new captain is bald? And old?"
- "No captain will ever replace Kirk."
- "A new Enterprise? Are you kidding me?"

Yet eventually, Picard won fans over. The new series became a fan favorite for most, and the errors of season one were quickly forgiven, as the principle philosophy of Trek continued to be central to the plots. The show had several things in common with TOS that made it viable with fans:

- The series was episodic rather than serial in nature. Miss an episode? No biggie. You can watch it later, but that won't affect your understanding of next week's show.
- A diverse crew was organized around one central character who epitomized the Federation and fought for the values of Starfleet.
- The central figure was a captain.
- Much of the conflict didn't happen on the ship but within and around the alien races. Overall, the crew was fairly harmonious.
- The show consisted of stories first, but that often dealt with deeper issues as a part of a singular plot. If you didn't like the topic or style of this week's episode, you might like what happens next week.

The political climate was also different at that time, and we will address that in a moment. But the divide moved again. The next time the New Trek vs. Old Trek reared its head was with the release of *Voyager*, and then likely the least liked series by fans, *Enterprise*. While DS9 was at initially as kind of limited in scope since everything happened in a single location, many fans didn't like it at first either. However, since it ran at the same time as *Voyager*, fans didn't complain too much.

But at that time, New Trek meant anything post TNG. Old Trek included TNG and TOS. Then, as is wont to happen, things changed yet again, and made a bigger shift this time.

The line for Old Trek vs. New Trek moved to the Kelvin timeline films on the new side, everything before that on the old. Janeway became a Trek hero, especially to female fans, who finally saw themselves represented at the Captain level. Sisko proved worthy as a leader, and some (but not all, and certainly not me) forgave Enterprise its trespasses against the Trek universe.

In this case, canon changed due to the introduction of yet another prequel to TOS, but this one in an alternate universe, leaving the canvas wide open for change.

Finally, when Discovery first aired in 2017, it polarized fans yet again, and for some fans, the line between New and Old Trek moved once again. Others still clung to the previous divisions, as we will see, and as of this writing and other new series emerge, it appears yet another divide may happen. But let's look at why this happens and why some of the divisions work and others don't.

THE POST-RODDENBERRY ARGUMENT (AND WHY IT FAILS)

So an easy divide would be the passing of Gene Roddenberry and, therefore, the end to his involvement with the series creatively. Many would argue that his legacy lived on, at least for a while, and yet others would argue that his influence ended well before his passing, and therefore the post-Roddenberry era started much earlier.

But I don't think it works for canon or as a dividing line between old and new Trek. Films were already set to be released, and Roddenberry had already shared his opinion of them, both good and bad, as we outlined above.

We also see that as he developed TNG, sometimes Roddenberry's views had evolved from TOS. To say that anything post-Roddenberry is New Trek and pre-Roddenberry is Old Trek clearly breaks down.

I also think earlier divisions just don't work. We are well past the TOS vs. TNG debate for most fans. Picard is just as great (or greater according to some) a captain as Kirk at least until we revisit him in the truly New Trek, Picard. But more on that in a moment.

However, the further we get from that debate and the closer we edge to the present, the more valid arguments for the New vs. Old Trek divides get.

VOYAGER, ENTERPRISE, AND DS9

In my mind, these shows are Old Trek, at least at this point in history. I have to admit that I never was, and likely never will be, a fan of Enterprise. Scott Bakula, while he is a great actor, will just never fit exactly as a Starfleet Captain. However, I must admit that despite my own prejudice, many fans have come to at least give the show a hall pass, if not some love, as a part of Trek history.

There is a reason for this though. First, Voyager, Enterprise, and until the final season, DS9 followed an episodic format. DS9 much more embraced the slow burn and was the first Trek show to really try that method. While Voyager had some lengthy episodes and some that could have been longer ("Year of Hell" anyone?), it was a bunch of self-contained stories with the overall goal of making it home.

The other difference? Old Trek, in this case, was about hope. It had heart and was multi-cultural (maybe even a little over the top in this area). Old Trek was also, for the most part, anti-war. War was always portrayed as bad.

The other difference was Old Trek's relationship with the past: yes, there were mistakes made, but we could learn from them. It showed us what humanity used to be, what we were before, and then presented a future that showed us what we could be. That kind of hope for culture and humanity resonated with the politics and atmosphere of the times.

Sure, America arrogantly strode around the globe defending peace and democracy regardless of how much the war machine to do so might cost. But we could learn and do better, right? Yes, we would still fail from time to time, and both Kirk and Picard are shown to be human and do just that. Sisko even embraces his humanity, and in the end, we grow to love him as a person.

A new divide came, however, and it changed everything for fans. But it, too, was and is a reflection of the world we live in.

THE NEW NEW TREK (AND WHY IT'S SO DIVISIVE)

The Kelvin timeline opened with a Federation at war, the planet Vulcan destroyed, and a much more emotional Mr. Spock. The line between right and wrong became much more rigid, and the desire to validate the right no matter what took precedent. Rather than trying to win over and change the intolerant, the Federation declared war on it.

In short, Trek became intolerant of the intolerant, and rather than trying to understand their viewpoint with heart, that heart was replaced with frustration and even a misguided, though perhaps well deserved, version of hate.

It's understandable. We live in a society that is not doing better. Many minorities have been fighting for so long for acknowledgment, equality, and respect that they are frustrated. Hope seems futile, and understandably so. So rather than building on the past showcasing the mistakes, we can learn from, the new Trek seeks to destroy that past, erase it, and start fresh.

Rather than avoiding war, something we cannot always do in the real world, the New Trek seeks out war in the name of "progress." And if we look at the history of humanity, that type of approach almost always ends with someone being oppressed and marginalized. It leaves chaos and destruction in its wake, things that take years to overcome, if it happens at all. Instead of working to learn from human history and improve on it, New Trek seems to adopt the same type of colonial imperialism that has been going on for centuries rather than embracing a new path.

For many Trek fans, they clearly see this as the opposite of Roddenberry's intent and indeed the antithesis of *The Tao of Trek*. While a generation that is understandably angry about the neglect of diversity and even outright racism and abuse is drawn to this type of Trek, the key for creators is to design stories with hope for a different tomorrow.

The issue with history is that often, the oppressed change roles and become the oppressor. Think of the persecution of Christians under the Roman Empire until Christianity became the state religion. Then those who would not convert to Christianity were tortured in the same way Christians were previously.

This is the pattern Old Trek seeks to break. We embark on peaceful explorations, not to take over new planets, mine them for what is valuable, press the original inhabitants into laboring for us, or even move them to remote and hostile parts of the planet, while we take over the more fertile and desirable areas. These hostile takeovers and the desire for freedom from oppression and taxation are the reasons the Revolutionary War happened, only to see Americans become the hostile explorers in the west, displacing the Native American tribes and waging war, moving them to reservations, and attempting to "civilize" them.

What Old Trek has shown us is that being civilized is not about how much a race of beings is like us, but how they have organized their own society. We need to respect those differences and even embrace and learn from them. TOS certainly did not do this perfectly, nor did TNG, but they did better than the Kelvin timeline films and even Discovery.

THE HOPE FOR NEW TREK

Does all that mean there is no hope for New Trek? Far from it. Let's look at some of what is happening now, and then in the next chapter, we will talk about the Trek of tomorrow and what hope that future might hold.

First, let's look at a couple of series running as of the writing of this book. While the very mention of *Picard* ignites some controversy among fans, overall, it has been received favorably. Why? Well, Patrick Stewart perhaps said it best when he warned fans ahead of time that this was not the same world as TNG:

"The world of TNG was one that felt too benevolent and safeguarded, and the universe is not quite so sugarcoated as we might have believed," he stated. "*Star Trek: Picard* is a response to the world of Brexit and Donald Trump and feeling, 'Why hasn't the Federation changed? Why hasn't Starfleet changed?' Maybe they're not as reliable and trustworthy as we all thought."

This seems to echo the sentiment that *Star Trek* needs to change with society as we change. It's true, the world is not as benevolent and sugarcoated as TOS and TNG made it out to be. There are actually evil actors out there, bent on doing evil things. People do not always act with the good of the many in mind, as great an idea as that might be.

In fact, we see in our world those who act in extreme self-interest with greed and self-interest taking precedent over the good of society. The difference in New Trek is that we portray that evil not only in the alien, less developed races the crew encounters but in humanity itself.

It's a mirror that, for some fans, betrays the idea that as humanity evolves and moves forward, we will get better at all of these things, and our morality will evolve at the same pace with technology and other advancements.

Lower Decks offers yet another view of humanity and Starfleet, although perhaps a more nuanced one than *Picard* or *Discovery*. The episodic nature of the show also appeals to fans, and for some, it epitomizes the resurgence of Old Trek.

The same can be said for *Prodigy*, the collaboration between Disney and Nickelodeon. While designed for kids, there are a lot of throwback Easter eggs that thrill longtime fans, and the themes of the show have given many of them hope for the resurgence of the themes of Old Trek.

What does that mean for the Trek of Tomorrow? Well, we think that fans can make a huge difference in what that looks like.

CHAPTER 17
THE TREK OF TOMORROW

"There's still much to do; still so much to learn. Mr. La Forge – engage!"

— Captain Picard

"You may find that having is not so pleasing a thing as wanting. This is not logical, but it is often true."

-- Mr. Spock, *"Amok Time"*

"Change is the essential process of all existence."

-- Mr. Spock, *"Let That Be Your Last Battlefield"*

A s of this writing, there are a lot of things ahead for Trek, and we can only hope that there is even more on the horizon. A new generation has embraced the values and the ideas of Trek, and they are watching with eager eyes as new crews on new ships boldly goes into brave new worlds. We talked about a few of these at the start of this book, but they bear repeating here.

There are times when those of us in love with Old Trek bemoan the loss of a show about exploration more than one about battles across the stars, and fortunately for us, we are being heard.

As we pen this chapter, Picard Season 2 has yet to air, although it starts soon on Paramount Plus. Season 3 has been written and is in production with an uncertain release date. One of the most anticipated series, one we know too little about. We do know that it is promised to return to more of the positive outlook for humanity reminiscent of TOS, but it will be serialized to foster the development of character story arcs.

Short Treks suspended filming when COVID-19 struck. The series of 10–20-minute shorts paralleled *Discovery* and featured characters from it and other series. The series was well received and even won an Emmy. There are plans to continue the series, but there is no word on when this will happen, if at all.

Yet another offshoot, *Star Fleet Academy*, is also in development. The primary showrunner for all of these is Alex Kurtzman, a fan favorite who is also reported to be someone fans love to hate. He's behind *Discovery*, the new *Picard*, and more expansions of the *Star Trek* world.

Finally, there is yet another controversial *Star Trek* spinoff in the works, or at least reportedly so as of this writing. It is fronted by *Discovery* star Michelle Yeoh and follows her work in Section 31, the covert intelligence arm of Starfleet first introduced in DS9.

"I don't want to see another Trek series about war or violence," one fan told me when sharing their thoughts on the series. "So no, as much as I liked Michelle Yeoh in her role, I don't think I am anticipating this series."

So what are fans anticipating?

THE CONTINUING SERIES

Paramount+ (CBS/Viacom) had doubled down and bet big on *Star Trek* and the future of many of the series. *Discovery* has been renewed for seasons 4 and 5. *Lower Decks* will see a season 4. *Prodigy* will continue with "Season 1B" later in 2022. *Strange New Worlds* has been greenlit for a second season before the first one even airs.

For the most part, these series will be tied to Paramount+ streaming service, and like other streaming services, unique content not available elsewhere is certainly part of what drives subscriptions.

There are those fans who don't want to pay extra to see series like *Discovery* and others, but for the most part, fans are willing to take the plunge for their Trek fix.

This isn't a philosophy book to discuss the future of television and streaming; however, we do recognize that this is an ongoing discussion. The future of television, whether streaming services, some new form of cable, or services that offer several subscriptions in one place, will likely emerge.

WILL *STAR TREK* RETURN TO THE BIG SCREEN?

With all of the controversy around *Star Trek* of late and the New Trek vs. Old Trek debate, the question of whether Trek will return to the big screen is a big one. After all, the last theater film in the series was released in 2016, and that's almost an entire film era between releases at this point.

However, Paramount is trying to build the franchise into something attractive for a new generation, and they have told us multiple times that a new Trek film will be on the way in 2023. What is it?

For now, we have no idea. But *Star Trek: Subtitle Unknown* remains a mystery. Will there be more films after that? Almost certainly. Will they be Discovery spinoffs? New takes on the Kelvin timeline? Even animated? We're left to guessing here.

What we would like to see:

- A *Lower Decks* film. I mean, this is the Trekkiest of Trek shows, so why not a big-screen debut?
- A *Prodigy* film. Well, if this takes off like I think it should. It would introduce a whole new generation of kids to the show.
- A final *Picard* showing on the big screen. Hey, I know Stewart is getting older, but come on! One more big-screen adventure would be awesome!
- Maybe a *Strange New Worlds* film. If this "yet-another-prequel" lives up to expectations and embraces the positive nature of TOS in the ways we hope, then I would love to see a big-screen adaptation.

What's really next? We can only hope those who make decisions at Paramount will listen to us, the fans. And that leads me to one final point.

FANS AND THE FUTURE OF TREK

Look, Trek would have been a forgotten, canceled show in space if it hadn't been for a dedicated group of fans. From letter-writing campaigns to support that made the show a success in syndication to the creation of fan-attended cons now famous the world over, fans have always driven the future of Trek.

Fan-created work, sometimes allowed by Paramount, other times squashed with impunity, has also driven the growth of fandom. From novelizations to film, from related books like this one to leadership books and others that speak to the true philosophy behind Trek and the inspiration its characters and cast have offered us over the years, it's all come from the fans.

In fact, while most of the cast of TOS is either gone or beyond making action adventure space films, they have left a legacy of greatness and some large shoes to fill. Many of the current showrunners are longtime fans, and while we may disagree with their interpretation of *The Tao of Trek* from time to time, we have to embrace it too. For the very fact that others don't always see things the way we do is at the very heart of *The Tao of Trek*.

Are the ranks of Trekkies growing or shrinking? That is a debate long asked, never truly answered except in the enduring popularity of the series. *Star Trek Discovery* has divided fans, *Picard* seems to unite them. Other films and series seem to do some of each. New Trekkies emerge, old Trekkies get, well, old. And the cycle continues.

Will it ever stop? At the moment, it seems the answer is "no." But as the saying goes, "It's hard to predict things. Especially when it comes to the future."

What is next? Well, we, as Trekkies, encourage you to look at *The Tao of Trek* as more than a book, more than an examination of philosophy, and look at it as a lifestyle. For, in the end, *The Tao of Trek* has little meaning unless it changes us and changes the world around us. The Tao is meant to be lived.

CHAPTER 18

THE TAO IS MEANT TO BE LIVED, NOT JUST READ

Any book on philosophy has two missions, really. One is to inspire thought and consideration and hopefully enable readers to come to some logical conclusion about some basic principles. Of course, the next step is the testing of those principles against the real world and determining how practical they actually are.

The greatest parts of philosophy are things that can be logically applied to every situation every single day. This is why most philosophies, including this one, fall short. Such an ambition is, in and of itself, impractical. For every rule, there will be an exception.

We don't have to look far into the Trek world to see this illustrated. The good of the many clearly does not always outweigh the good of the few or the one. At least not in practice. The Prime Directive or General Order One turns out to be more of a guideline than an actual rule. It's simply beyond the capacity of explorers to never mix a bit of colonialism in there.

But I digress. We have already covered those topics extensively. What we need is to determine where we go from here.

While I am not a religious guy, one of my all-time favorite Catholic priests sums up how I feel (and perhaps why I am not a religious guy). "The mass is made to be lived, not just observed," he says.

So we will apply the same thinking to *The Tao of Trek*: this Tao is not just meant to be read, celebrated, or observed. It is meant to be lived. On that note, here are my takeaways.

DEVELOP YOUR OWN PRIME DIRECTIVE

The most important thing you will ever determine is why you are here on this planet. What your purpose is. Your "why." Then your job is to use it to make the world a better place. And make no mistake, that includes your own world. Whether you embrace your passion as a hobby that enriches your life or somehow find a way to make a living at it, your why matters.

My grandmother made quilts. She made them for everyone, sometimes more than one. If you got married, had a birthday, had a child, or whatever reason, she would make you a quilt. The same applied whether you were family or one of her many friends.

Of course, that was not my grandmother's only why. She did many other things to enrich the world around her, and she found joy in those things. But quilting was one of them, and she brought joy to a lot of people through doing so.

I would argue that there was a more profound why at work. I write to entertain but also to educate and provide an escape for those who need a reprieve from their ordinary lives. It's my why. The what is writing stories and books like this one.

What is your why? What is your core motivation for the things you do? What is the one "rule" of your life that reigns over everything else, fuels your desires, and makes your heart happy?

You can call that what you will, but for now, I will simply call it your Prime Directive. Your General Order Number One. The *Enterprise* was built for the purpose of exploration. What were you built for?

When you find it, follow it. You won't live life with no regrets: anyone who promises you such nonsense is selling something. But you will be happier in the long run if, more often than not, you let your Prime Directive guide your behavior.

EMBRACE INFINITE DIVERSITY IN INFINITE COMBINATIONS

As I write these words, it feels like there is nothing I can say that will do this principle justice. Currently, we live in a world divided by something as simple as the proper response to a pandemic and whether or not top scientists and politicians are lying to us.

The United States and much of the world are largely divided on other issues as well. Some of them matter more than others. For example, when it comes to human rights issues, I cannot in good conscience abide by the opinions of those who seek to take away those rights from others. The abuses like the ones happening in China and other countries around the world are certainly not something we want to embrace.

But there are issues that are not as clear-cut. In the U.S., we struggle with topics like gun control, police brutality, homelessness, poverty, and more. Many of these are nuanced topics filled with talk of individual responsibility vs. the duty of society to care for those less fortunate who are a part of it. Gun control does not mean the same thing in Chicago or the suburbs of L.A. as it does in rural Idaho, where guns are sometimes essential for survival and even hunting to feed one's family.

Then there are others still that, born out of fear or hatred from another age, tend to dominate headlines when they happen. Racial inequality and even abuse, the marginalizing of the LBTQ+ community, and other debates rage both publicly and privately. Not all of them are divided along political party lines, but some are, and we have let the colors red and blue represent us in ways they probably should not.

Troy: Through all the social media hype and arguments I have seen and sometimes unwittingly participated in, I've discovered there is really only one thing I can do: control my own reaction to them.

I can embrace infinite diversity in infinite combinations. In doing so, I recognize the rights of all humanity and, in a larger sense, all sentient beings I may never meet in this lifetime. I acknowledge their right to life, to freedom as long as exercising such freedom does not bring harm to another or themselves, and the pursuit of happiness with the same caveat.

For my freedom ends where it impinges on the freedom of others, and all such freedom comes with responsibility and potential consequences. Just because I can do something does not mean I should, as my quilt-making grandmother would say.

Such rights are not mine alone. They belong to everyone regardless of race, religious affiliation or creed, sexual orientation, gender, skin tone, height, weight, or any other such metric by which prejudice could be introduced.

James: While I was raised in a racist and biased culture, I try to fight against it in my own mind. One way I do is starting conversations with people different than me and asking about their beliefs or experiences. Listening to someone discuss racism from the point of view of a black man is both fascinating and educational. Hearing a woman discuss sexism in her life gives real context to how far we haven't come. Discussing what it means to be gay with a gay man or woman informs you in ways you would never imagine.

Asking anyone to explain anything they know more about than you is a wonderful thing. They will feel heard, you will feel educated. Don't argue with them, though you can say things like "I never knew that." Just let your world view expand as you learn more about the infinite diversity around you.

The thing is this: if enough of us do this and embrace this part of *The Tao of Trek*, we can change the world and the world beyond when we get there.

CONSIDER THE NEEDS OF THE MANY

There are some topics I could rant about for days, and perhaps the application of this principle of the Tao is one of them. We live in a society filled with greed that talks a lot about self-care with no idea of what that actually means. Most of us, much of the time, are selfish. We put not only our own needs first, but our wants too. We don't stop to consider the needs of the many who surround us.

A simple example is the concentration of wealth. In the United States, this is especially egregious. The top 10% of the nation's wealthy control 70% of the wealth in the United States. 70%! We've all heard the arguments for the trickle-down economy, but as long as there is human greed involved, this does not work.

And when we see corporations where the CEO makes more in a day or even an hour than the average worker in the company does in a year, that means there is an imbalance. Clearly, many of those in the top 10% are not working for the good of the many.

This is not to say that some of them are not more generous than others. This is certainly true, and I am sure that I will get some mail to that effect once this book is released and read. But the fact that such individuals are noteworthy only serves to prove my point: if someone wealthy giving money away makes news, or being generous with their employees, or some similar thing, it tells us something.

The news media only reports on the noteworthy, not the mundane. Seldom does a report of a sunny, average weather day get the press of a tornado, hurricane, or another storm. The reason is simple: such events are significant in that they differ from the norm. Since the norm is to horde one's wealth and hang onto it for one's own benefit, generosity has become news.

But it goes beyond that. Studies show that many people, though they support the idea of government programs to bolster the health of the poor, offer them income assistance, and even institute other programs, few want to pay the requisite taxes that would be required of them for that to happen.

In fact, while most people expect the government to "do something" when a natural disaster strikes or there is a homelessness crisis like the one we are experiencing now, almost none of them would vote for a tax increase to fund such endeavors, nor would they donate their own money to a private cause.

In addition, charities that take the money of donors and don't do the good with them that they promised also abound. Even in charity, greed and avarice can be found if one looks hard enough.

That sounds bleak, right? But there is good news. You see, change begins with one person. Then another, and another. The more people who break this cycle who begin to look at life not as a game they need to win but as a vehicle to make the world a better place, even if it means personal sacrifice from time to time, the greater our world will be.

And the only person I can control is me and my own generosity whenever possible. And the only person you can control is you and your ability to see the needs of the many whenever possible.

This, too, is hard. Much like the other parts of the Tao, it is both aspirational and ideal. But if we resolve to try, we can do better. That is one of the ways we can put the Tao into practice.

BOLDLY GO

One of the biggest obstacles to accomplishment and to living in the way the Tao asks us to is fear. We hoard wealth for fear that if we give it up now, we may need it later. We avoid kindness for fear it will be abused or that it will not be returned to us. And we fail to follow our dreams because we fear failure.

Trust me, I (Troy) have been there. Let me share a personal story: in 2001, I was headed back from a friend's house in Wilhoit, Arizona. I'd ridden down there to pick up a motorcycle tank he'd painted for me.

It was a cold day, and while often I rode with short sleeves (still gloves and boots, always a helmet) that day, I had opted for a heavy flannel, jeans, and extra layers. Good thing. Because as I neared Prescott on the way to my home in Chino Valley at the time, up ahead, I saw a Toyota truck waiting to turn into a subdivision.

The sun was at my back, my headlight was on, and I swore the driver saw me and hesitated. But she didn't, clearly. I hit the side of a Toyota at 45 miles per hour. To cut a long story short, I could have died that day, but I didn't. You can call what saved me whatever you want: God, angels, luck combined with some skill, the doctors and hospital staff, whatever you wish. I have my own opinions, which I will keep to myself, at least in this context.

Something changed that day, though. A near-death experience altered my perspective. It took me a bit, but not too long after that, I embarked on finding a way to pursue my dream of a writing career. The fear that held me back kind of took a back seat. Because what if I died and never had a chance to fulfill that dream, not for lack of opportunity, but for lack of movement?

Maybe you feel the same. Maybe there is something in your Prime Directive, your why, that you truly want to follow but haven't because of fear. Maybe it is time to let that fear go, or maybe it is past time. But it is never too late.

To live the Tao, you will have to do more than think about these ideas. You're going to have to act on them. You're going to have to boldly go into life from this day forward. Because each of us has our own mission, our own things to seek, our own path to walk.

And as they say, "Fortune favors the brave."

LIVE LONG AND PROSPER

And so, we have come to the end. The end of an exploration of a universe that, like our own, is ever-expanding. We haven't yet reached the point of an end where we can say there is no more. Time marches on; the world evolves, we reach for the stars and beyond. And as we evolve, so does *The Tao of Trek*.

Sometimes it resonates and follows the precepts set forth by its creator, Gene Roddenberry. Other times, it falls short or even seems to turn against them. That is because just as we orchestrate and write the chapters of our own lives, we make mistakes. We are human. And so are those who interpret the vision of what *Star Trek* is and what it was meant to be.

When does peaceful exploration descend into war? When will we overcome prejudice against other races, other species, those who are different than we are? When will we apply technology to solving the world's problems with scarcity rather than pushing into the ever-growing military armaments and advancements? When will we grow beyond the boundaries of our frail societies to something better?

Or is the world of Trek simply one that is both aspirational and unattainable? Will we reach for the stars as yet another place to conquer and dominate, or a place to be explored, discovered, and understood?

This book is not long enough or great enough to provide those answers. For that, we will have to keep living, following *The Tao of Trek* the best that we can. But before we go, there is one small thing we want to offer, one final blessing.

Live Long and Prosper. Peace be upon you. Until next time.

CHAPTER 19
TAO OF TREK REFERENCES

1. Ralph Senensky, Is There In Truth No Beauty? 2011.
2. Shatner, William. *Star Trek* Memories, October 1993.
3. Leonard Nimoy, I Am Spock, 1995.
4. https://www.hollywoodreporter.com/movies/movie-news/they-didnt-get-it-first-star-trek-movie-almost-killed-franchise-1258930/
5. Paula Block, VCP Senior Director of Licensed Publishing, TrekBBS posts, December 2005.
6. Leonard Nimoy, I Am Not Spock, 1975.
7. Hinds, Jane (1997). "The Wrath of Ahab; or, Herman Melville Meets Gene Roddenberry". The Journal of American Culture. 20 (1): 43–46.
8. Okuda, Michael; Denise Okuda (1996). *Star Trek* Chronology: The History of the Future, revised edition.
9. Kraemer, Ross Shepard; William Cassiday; Susan Schwartz (2003). Religions of *Star Trek*. Basic Books. p. 164.
10. https://www.cinemablend.com/television/2571876/star-trek-creator-gene-roddenberry-impact-felt-most-new-tv-shows-rod-roddenberry

11. "Charter of the United Nations". United Nations. 26 June 1945.

12. Simpson, Gerry (2006). Great Powers and Outlaw States: Unequal Sovereigns in the International Legal Order.

13. Richard J. Peltz, "On a Wagon Train to Afghanistan: Limitations on *Star Trek*'s Prime Directive", University of Arkansas at Little Rock Law Review, Volume 25, Issue 3, Article 6, 2003.

14. Gene Roddenberry, interviewed by Marc Cushman in 1982 and 1990 and quoted in These Are The Voyages: TOS -- Season 3.

15. https://www.hollywoodreporter.com/tv/tv-news/star-trek-how-discovery-brought-faith-franchise-1178661/

16. The Economics of *Star Trek*: The Proto-Post-Scarcity Economy: Fifth Anniversary Edition, Webb, Rick, 11 February 2019.

17. https://fanfilmfactor.com/2020/09/14/i-figured-out-the-secret-of-star-trek-lower-decks-and-its-gonna-blow-your-mind-and-make-you-love-this-show-editorial/

18. Shatner, William, Leonard: My Fifty-Year Friendship With a Remarkable Man, Thomas Dunne Books; 2016.

19. https://www.startrek.com/article/the-jewish-ritual-that-led-nimoy-to-create-the-vulcan-salute

20. Alien Language Department, The Vulcan Language Guide, April Publications, January 1, 1977

21. Kagan, Janet, Uhura's Song, Pocket Books, January 1985.

22. https://blog.sivanaspirit.com/dudeism-buddhism-big-lebowski/

23. Roberts, Wess, Make it So: Leadership Lessons from *Star Trek* the *Next Generation*, Gallery Books, August 1996.

24. https://www.nytimes.com/1998/05/02/nyregion/studio-sues-over-a-star-trek-book.html

25. https://www.forbes.com/sites/peterdecherney/2016/05/02/in-copyright-lawsuit-star-trek-fan-work-gets-its-easy-rider-moment/?sh=48da82ac5fdc

26. https://www.youtube.com/watch?v=1W1_8IV8uhA
27. https://www.hollywoodreporter.com/business/business-news/judge-makes-big-ruling-sending-star-trek-fan-film-dispute-jury-trial-960703/
28. https://fanfilmfactor.com/2020/07/31/gary-graham-leaves-the-axanar-project/
29. https://www.emergencyfirstresponse.com/good-samaritan-laws-and-cpr/

ABOUT JAMES T. LAMBERT

James T. Lambert writes science-fiction, urban fantasy, and a little steampunk from his writing office/land yacht 'Bertrude'. By day he breaks carefully constructed code conceived by clever coders, while by night he sorts strings of syllibant sentences for story structure. Since his first novel-length project in the 2011 NaNoWriMo, he's been polishing his craft, working toward his overnight success after ten years. Other than writing and breaking things, Jim also enjoys reading, movies, comics, theater, boardgames, Scotch, craft beer, hot air ballooning, and having far too many hobbies.

ABOUT TROY L. LAMBERT

Troy Lambert is a freelance writer and mystery suspense author from Boise, Idaho where he lives with the love of his life and some very talented dogs. When he is not staring at a screen plagiarizing the alphabet, he can be found outside, hiking, camping, riding his bike, skiing, or generally enjoying the outdoors. You can find his other work on his website.

If you enjoyed this book, you might also enjoy *Stray Ally*, a book about a man who finds a dog in the wilderness and saves him. In the end, the dog proves to be truly the man's Stray Ally, proving that dogs are indeed man's best friend.

Made in the USA
Middletown, DE
30 April 2022

64981494R00116